Bite by Bite

American History Through Feasts, Foods, and Side Dishes

Marc Aronson and Paul Freedman

with contributions from

Frederick Douglass Opie   Tatum Willis

Amanda Palacios   David Zheng

Illustrated by Toni D. Chambers

 Atheneum Books for Young Readers
NEW YORK LONDON TORONTO SYDNEY NEW DELHI

atheneum

ATHENEUM BOOKS FOR YOUNG READERS · An imprint of Simon & Schuster Children's Publishing Division · 1230 Avenue of the Americas, New York, New York 10020 · Text © 2024 by Marc Aronson and Paul Freedman · Jacket illustration © 2024 by Toni D. Chambers · Interior illustration © 2024 by Toni D. Chambers · All rights reserved, including the right of reproduction in whole or in part in any form. · ATHENEUM BOOKS FOR YOUNG READERS is a registered trademark of Simon & Schuster, LLC. Atheneum logo is a trademark of Simon & Schuster, LLC. · Simon & Schuster: Celebrating 100 Years of Publishing in 2024 · For information about special discounts for bulk purchases, please contact Simon & Schuster Special Sales at 1-866-506-1949 or business@simonandschuster.com. · The Simon & Schuster Speakers Bureau can bring authors to your live event. For more information or to book an event, contact the Simon & Schuster Speakers Bureau at 1-866-248-3049 or visit our website at www.simonspeakers.com. · The text for this book was set in Urge Text. · The illustrations for this book were rendered digitally. · Manufactured in the United States of America · 0424 BVG · First Edition · 10 9 8 7 6 5 4 3 2 1 · Library of Congress Cataloging-in-Publication Data · Names: Aronson, Marc, author. | Freedman, Paul, author. · Title: Bite by bite : American history through feasts, foods, and side dishes / Marc Aronson and Paul Freedman with contributions from Frederick Douglass Opie, Amanda Palacios, Tatum Willis, David Zheng. · Description: First edition. | New York : Atheneum Books for Young Readers, [2024] | Includes bibliographical references. | Audience: Ages 10 and up | Summary: "A middle-grade nonfiction book cowritten by Marc Aronson and historian/food writer Dr. Paul Freedman and with contributors Dr. Frederick Douglass Opie, Tatum Willis, Amanda Palacios, and David Zheng. American food and, by extension, American identify is much broader than the phrase "as American as apple pie." In a series of meals that take readers from pre-1492 through today, the text explores this country's identify and history through the lens of food, highlighting how cultures and histories mix to create the rich tapestry of America."— Provided by publisher. · Identifiers: LCCN 2023003084 | ISBN 9781665935500 (hardcover) | ISBN 9781665935524 (ebook) · Subjects: LCSH: Food—United States—History—Juvenile literature. | Food habits—United States—History—Juvenile literature. | United States—History—Juvenile literature. · Classification: LCC TX360.U6 A76 2024 | DDC 394.1/20973—dc23/eng/20230320 · LC record available at https://lccn.loc.gov/2023003084

To every librarian fighting for young people's
right to read, learn, explore, and think
—M. A.

For Caleb, Lila, Alfred, and Joshua
—P. F.

CONTENTS

INTRODUCTION

If you were a visitor from outer space
and got your sense of the United States from commercials, you
might think all we ate were burgers loaded with bacon and cheese
or pizzas topped with curling islands of pepperoni. Millions of
burgers and pies are sold each year. But what if your own favorites are never advertised as typical American food? Where did
pizza and burgers come from, anyway? How do we get a real
sense of the many kinds of food we enjoy? And what do those
food choices say about all of us? Take the phrase *As American
as . . .* apple pie (an English dessert with European and Turkish
roots not considered typically American until the 1920s), hot
dogs (German), corn on the cob (Mexican), Thanksgiving turkey
(venison and eel were far more important to the Pilgrims). These
old and mistaken images of all-American favorites assumed that
one kind of family in one neighborhood with one taste stood for
all of us. That was never true.

What is American food? It depends on who is asking and when you have the conversation. In the early 1900s, Italian immigrants were warned not to persist in eating the pastas and tomato sauces of their homeland because they were not good for you, but now pizza is second only to burgers (named after Hamburg, Germany) in national popularity. At one time you could eat Mexican food only in the Southwest and try Chinese foods just in major cities on the East or West Coast. Today it may be easier for you to find a chain selling tacos or orange chicken than a diner (originally called "night wagons," as they were stationed near factories and served workers between shifts) offering grilled cheese sandwiches and, well, apple pie.

What we eat tells us where we live, how we move from place to place, how we grow our foods, and which advertisements we see. If we look carefully at how different Americans have gathered ingredients and then cooked and shared meals, we really can see many of the key stories in American history—laid out for us bite by bite.

Generally, and mistakenly, the history of the United States begins on the East Coast with the failed Roanoke Colony or with Jamestown in 1607 and the arrival of enslaved Africans in 1619. Historians have long known that the first people to arrive in the Americas came from what is now Siberia in Russia. Experts endlessly debate exactly who those new arrivals were, where they came from before arriving in Siberia, and when they crossed over. But we do know that human settlement in the Americas—and thus the true sources of American food—began more than ten, perhaps twenty thousand years before 1607, in the Pacific

Northwest. Then the first great transformation of American food—the arrival of corn—took place thousands of years before the Europeans arrived. European and African contact with North Americans—and thus more and new forms of American food—moved from the south to the north, through the southwest, nearly a century before Jamestown. If not for the success of the Haitians in defeating first British and then French armies, the center of North America might well have been French-speaking, with the English trapped on the Atlantic coast. In the 1800s each wave of immigration to North America added new questions, debates, and choices to the American kitchen and table.

This book treats the "Englishness" of American food, culture, and society as a constantly contested question, one we still debate today. Looking carefully at food gives us the chance to uncover the true histories of the many Americans and Americas.

PART ONE

FIRST FOODS— FOUNDATIONS

Celilo Falls:
First Salmon Feast
10,000 BCE to Today

To begin this pageant of food, North America, and history, we need to start where it all began: the Pacific Northwest. Carefully studying the DNA in ancient skeletons and working closely with modern Native American peoples, scientists have assembled some of the key pieces in the story of how humans first came to the Americas. At one time the land connecting what are now the Americas and Russia was a large, wide, and open area. This was not a narrow "bridge" but rather a reasonable place to live—when much of the nearby land was covered in ice. Scholars call the land now entirely submerged underwater "Beringia." Some of the more restless, though, did leave and spread down the coast on foot or by boat, the first to enter the new continent. Whether they slowly walked the strips of land between sea and ice or more rapidly rode the waters in and out of the jagged coastline, they came to, and through, the Pacific Northwest. Some chose to stay and settle there. For more than ten thousand years (and this could be at least fifteen to twenty thousand years), these first Americans built their lives around the meeting places of land and sea, hills, and rivers, near this coast. And so, this is our place to start.

Moving inland from the coast, you reach the Columbia River Plateau. There, the Columbia and Snake Rivers cut through a landscape that was created through massive lava flows millions of years ago. For the peoples of the plateau, the rivers provide fish, while in the higher elevations, there are animals to hunt and bushes whose roots and berries offer both tasty treats and medicines.

Tatum Willis is an enrolled member of the Confederated Tribes of the Umatilla Indian Reservation (CTUIR) and also descends from the Yakama, Nez Perce, and Oglala Lakota nations. The CTUIR include the Cayuse, the Umatilla, and the Walla Walla. The three separate groups each lived in their own distinct areas until recently. The Cayuse moved throughout the year in a wide circle through areas of what are now Washington, Oregon, and Idaho. The men were known as particularly brave and skilled horsemen and developed the distinct Cayuse pony. Disease, as well as conflicts with white newcomers and soldiers, diminished the Cayuse until, in 1855, they agreed to share a reservation with the Umatilla and the Walla Walla. Much of the distinct Cayuse language has been lost—so Tatum is studying Nez Perce, which is similar.

She recounted a version of the tale of how the Native people came to live along the rivers and inlets of the Pacific Northwest. Wishpoosh, the monster beaver, was killing the people and not letting them settle on the land and fish in the rivers. Coyote battled with Wishpoosh to protect the people and then fooled him by turning himself into a branch, which Wishpoosh swallowed, then turned back into himself and carved the beaver up from inside. Then he tossed the pieces, and each became one of the Native peoples of the area. As another version of the same story explains,

> From the head of Wishpoosh, Coyote made the Nez
>   Perces, great in council.
> From the arms, he made the Cayuses, powerful with
>   the bow and war club.
> From the legs, he made the Klickitats, famous runners.
> From the ribs, he made the Yakamas.

The people were placed in specific lands, which became their homes. In 1855, at the treaty council that created the Umatilla Indian Reservation, the Cayuse leader Ictixec said, "This is our mother, this country, as if we drew our living from her." More recently, an elder named Jim Yoke could still name 270 individual spots along the Cowlitz and Naches Rivers where Coyote had placed fish or berries, and defeated dangerous beings to prepare the land for the arrival of the people. "Hundreds of generations of ancestors," E. Thomas Morning Owl, general counsel of the CTUIR explains, "have known this land intimately from living on it for thousands of years. Every creek, spring, pond, swale, saddle, box canyon, draw, and peak witnessed our people's long history here, and our people knew all the features of this land." This sense of being deeply connected to a specific place defined their relationship to food.

Knowing the land, walking it, observing it, valuing it, the Native peoples treated the foods they gathered and hunted as part of their own living world. Plants and animals gave humans the gift of themselves, and the people in turn honored them. Food was not a packaged object; it was another life in a shared world. That does not mean the Native peoples had a limited diet—they also met to trade, which gave them access to favorite berries and roots, fish and meats that were not available in their lands. The center for trade along the Columbia River (which now separates Oregon from Washington) was Celilo Falls, home to the First Salmon Feast.

The CTUIR is about an hour and half away from Celilo, where the First Salmon Feast has been celebrated for thousands of years. Salmon are born inland, swim out to sea, then return upstream to lay their eggs in the same place where they were born. To reach the spawning grounds the fish needed to swim up the thundering waters of Celilo Falls. Virginia Beavert, a Yakama elder, recalled that:

> To me, the falls at Celilo were like a live human being.
> When we used to arrive at the Columbia River, you
>   could hear the sound of the waterfalls.
> The sound of the falls would envelop you and you
>   would become deaf.
> It's like the sound permeates your entire body.

In the 1950s the United States government decided to expand a decades-long project of dam-building on the Columbia River.

In order to provide electrical power—both for a growing population and for the expanding military-defense industries—and to manage water flow, they built a dam that destroyed the falls. While this was beneficial to many, it threatened and transformed a central event for the Indian peoples of the Pacific Northwest.

Chief Tommy Kuni Thompson led the very last feast held while the waters still cascaded over the rocks. He shared a description of a ceremony a few years before the dam with author Martha Ferguson McKeown. Here are some highlights of his account:

Tommy's adult son Henry sat on a wooden platform built over the falls, holding a long wooden pole with a net at the end. The first hint that salmon were coming would be flights of birds called mud swallows—for they arrive just ahead of the fish. Henry saw the mud swallows, still the salmon did not come. Soon Henry's place was taken by Tommy's young grandsons Richard and Davis, who managed to snag the first fish. Many more would follow. Women set up a long table next to the wooden house where everyone was to gather. As men brought in the catch, women scaled and cleaned the fish and prepared them to be cooked in the open air over wooden fires.

First the fish were split, then willow sticks were pushed up through the flesh to hold the salmon. Kettles filled with dried roots boiled on top of small black stoves. During the feast people would eat salmon, eel, roots, vegetables, and huckleberries— foods that the people had caught, gathered, or gained through trades for hundreds if not thousands of years.

The ceremony itself took place inside a big wooden house.

Chief Thompson circled from right to left as the world turned, asking for the meal to be blessed. Drummers began to play and lines of local Indians and guests waited to be fed.

"Our Father, we greet Thee," said Chief Thompson. "These children of earth come here to share our thanks today. We come to pay tribute to all hungry people in the name of the Great Almighty." After everyone took a sip of river water, he rang a bell, and the feast began.

Tatum was born long after the falls were dammed. But she knows the story of the falls well. "The Celilo First Salmon Feast usually occurs in spring, early April, and signifies the beginning of the fishing season. While these salmon feasts occur all over the Pacific Northwest, Celilo is a major event. The falls (or where they used to be) sit on the border of Oregon and Washington, and peoples of the great Columbia River Basin would have traveled there for this feast. Salmon, of course, would be the major component, usually roasted over a fire."

Janice Jones is a friend of Tatum's family and has attended many First Salmon Feasts. She explained that some aspects of the event have changed. The salmon is caught below the dam by Native fishermen and brought to the event. Instead of cooking it on sticks over an open fire, the men dig a pit and bake it in tinfoil. Seven (or at large events fourteen) drummers play, matching the days of the week. Once the feast begins, the foods are served in order—each matching the "time" in the season when it is ready. First salmon, then elk—small pieces, like jerky—then deer. After the meats come the roots, again in order: bitterroot or pyaxx̣í in Umatilla, biscuit-root or lúukš, and cous, followed by berries, huckleberries, and chokecherries. As the food is brought in, people thank the Creator in a sequence of songs.

One of the most important roots that has been harder to find in recent years—when local farmers have removed the root fields—is camas. Known as "the queen of the bulbs," camas appears aboveground as a spring herb but underground as a white bulb or root. In the moist prairie lands and damp meadows where camas flourishes, plentiful, blooming plants can "resemble lakes of fine, clear water." But Native peoples who did not have camas growing in their lands could only get it through trade—and many different peoples would gather at Celilo to exchange goods.

Eaten raw, camas is crisp and has little taste, like an uncooked potato, but when baked it becomes sweet—some describe the flavor as being between brown sugar and maple sugar. As Kanim Moses, a member of the CTUIR, told Tatum, camas "has to be cooked in the ground before we can eat it. But when it's done, it tastes like candy." Judith Moses, Tatum's aunt and Kanim's mother, added, "Camas is my favorite because of my grandma. We used to go digging for it with her while we were at church camp, not far from Kamiah [Idaho]. It's really easy to dig for, not like cous root. It's easy, soft ground. It reminds me of camping with my family, being with family. That side of the family still grows and processes it, particularly the men. They have a large pit dug into the ground, and they bake the camas in the big pit every year. That's the usual way to cook it. I want to go up there more to see it, but it's the same time as our huckleberry-picking time. Our gram would see that the camas was picked, make sure it was put away, then go out for huckleberry picking. Those old ladies always had something to do—pick one food, put it away, then head out for the next." Camas and huckleberries are just two of the roots and berries that have been grown locally or gained by trade. Others include bitterroot, wild onion, cous, wild carrot, soapberry, gooseberry, and sarvis berry.

The First Salmon Feast is still celebrated, though salmon has to be brought in from below the dam. The old format is still followed, but now there are more "Western" foods in addition to the traditional ones. And there are foods that get blended between the two, like huckleberry cake or huckleberry sauce poured over ice cream and fry bread.

The changes to the feast that the dam brought are just one part of how life in the area was affected. As Tatum puts it, "The early twentieth century and its technological advances led to hydroelectric dams being placed on the Columbia River. The area became known for its manufacturing, particularly making defense equipment for World War II. To this day a nearby town's high school mascot is the Bombers for their role in creating the atomic weapons dropped on Japan. In the late fifties the government decided to dam the river and flood Celilo Falls and The Dalles. Although fishing rights were supposedly protected by the treaties signed with the US government in the 1800s, Congress decreed that the flooding from the dam would not impede the fishing. They paid the tribes some millions for their loss and continued with the project." In fact, salmon runs have declined dramatically. Congress was forced to pay the tribes because their representatives came to Washington and pointed out that this decision directly broke the treaty signed in 1855. They were unable to save the falls, but at least won the point that Native peoples deserved to be compensated for their loss.

Damming the Celilo Falls placed the needs, desires, and policies of outsiders ahead of the traditions of Native peoples who had lived on the land for thousands of years. But that is not the end of the story. E. Thomas Morning Owl thinks the loss of the falls can be useful to Native people today: "The elders who are getting older and passing, the ones that were there, it really affected them. And those of us of the younger generation who've never seen it, it's basically in the stories. But until the 1970s, when the Native people began to stand up for their rights, the trade-off wasn't fair. It wasn't a balanced trade. So now the people are standing forward to protect their treaty rights on the river, and it helps to take (the destruction of the falls) as a guidepost for how we need to strengthen ourselves." (The story of the loss of the falls has been turned into the musical *The Ghosts of Celilo*, which can be viewed on YouTube.)

The efforts of Native peoples to fight for their rights are having an effect. In July of 2022, the Biden administration released a study on the poor condition of salmon in the Snake River and the costs of removing four dams along its span. Celilo was not among the selected sites, but the recognition of the damage the dams have done to salmon and the violation of the treaty rights of Native peoples is an important step. There is a chance that at least those four dams will be removed.

Now some Native people, such as Kanim Moses, are trying to return to the foods of their land, their waters, their ancestors: "We were the healthiest people before we stopped eating our first foods. Restoring first foods feels like restoring our health as a people."

The First Salmon Feast shows us history—from the first peoples in the Americas to the conflicts between them and later arrivals—and food that directly connect people with the water and land and animals where they live. Today the "farm-to-table" movement has spread across the country (see Chapter 12), and more and more Americans are seeking ways to "eat locally." We are rediscovering the wisdom of people whose foodways were based on the foods they grew and caught and understood from the air and soil, rivers, and hills in which they lived.

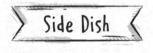

The Huckleberry

There are lots of edible berries in the wild that we rarely see in stores: cloudberries, gooseberries, currants. Huckleberries.

Wild plants like huckleberries cannot be cultivated because their roots are too shallow. The berries grow in much of the United States, especially in areas with a lot of moisture. That's why they're plentiful in the rainy Pacific Northwest. Huckleberries can be red, black, or blue. They are smaller and a bit more tart than blueberries, which they resemble.

Huckleberries are particularly important to the Salish and Kootenai people in the Flathead Reservation (Montana). The berries are gathered in summer and dried in order to be stored for winter. They are often used in soups and other cooked preparations and have a much more concentrated flavor than, for example, blueberries. Huckleberries are harvested after bitterroot and camas are harvested in the spring. They're also traditionally used as a heart medicine and for rheumatism.

Huckleberries are found out in the wild, and the name of Mark Twain's Huckleberry "Huck" Finn is associated with this wildness in the sense that his character is free and nonconforming. As Twain said about his friend Tom Blankenship, the model for Huck Finn, "His liberties were totally unrestricted. He was the only really independent person—boy or man—in the community." Similarly, in American slang, a "huckleberry" can mean an "unsophisticated person," a "hick." On the other hand, "I'm your huckleberry" used to mean "I'm the right person for this job."

Corn: The Invention That Transformed the Americas

Precontact to Today

The Native peoples of the Americas were great food scientists. Over countless generations they learned to take the plants they saw growing around them, improve them, plant them, harvest them, and turn them into the foods we know today as corn and potatoes, cassava and peanuts, tomatoes and chile peppers, chocolate and vanilla. Two of these—corn and chiles—take us to our next stop, the Southwest.

Corn is one of the world's most important inventions, for it does not exist in nature and was developed entirely by human beings. Somewhere in what is now Mexico, people noticed a small, wild grass called "teosinte" that had tiny, hard, and widely spaced kernels. Perhaps around 7000 BCE they had bred from teosinte a plant closer to modern corn that could be grown, harvested, and eaten. Those corn-ish crops were spread by trade and travel south to the Amazon and, later, west to the Andes. In the Amazon, another set of skilled farmers kept improving the plants, until by about four thousand years ago, the mixture of strains from Mexico and the Amazon produced a version similar to the corn we eat today. Though we cannot yet prove the link, right where and when Native people developed this hardy, healthy source of food, a series of great civilizations rose: the Olmec, the Maya, the Toltec, and the Aztec. Corn changed how people farmed, cooked, ate, and indeed lived throughout the Americas.

Anyone who wants to have corn as a food needs to learn how to plant it, nurture it, harvest it, and prepare for the next crop. Because the kernels are held inside a husk, corn cannot reseed itself—people must cultivate every single stalk. So, if we find ancient corncobs, we know that those who grew and ate them had been learning from others. Once corn knowledge spread, the peoples of the Americas had a reliable food, harvest after harvest. And, with the addition of a second innovation, corn became a staple food like no other because it is unusually nutritious and grows under a wide range of weather conditions.

In order to turn dried corn kernels into a dough that can be shaped into flat cakes such as tacos or tortillas, they must be mixed with ashes or lime or limestone—substances that give off alkalis. This process is still known by the term the Aztecs used, "nixtamalization." Corn contains niacin, a form of vitamin B that all human beings need. But our bodies can only access and absorb that crucial vitamin if corn has been nixtamalized. Nixtamalized corn is a perfect food—filling and nutritious in ways quite different from wheat or rice. Corn and knowledge of how to prepare it spread from Mexico as far north as Ottawa, as far east as Cape Cod, and as far west as Arizona. And with corn came new beliefs and perhaps new peoples.

Corn comes in a very wide variety of shapes, sizes, and flavors. That's because it was developed over such a long time and in different parts of the Americas. Most modern North Americans are accustomed to yellow, white, or bicolor versions that range between sweet and so sweet that in high summer, you can pick a cob and eat it while standing amid the rows of corn. That fresh, raw corn tastes like candy. In the Southwest, though, blue corn is more highly valued. The peoples of the Andes in South America like corn that has very large white kernels and softer "skin," and is less sweet. Some types of corn do especially well when dried, others when eaten fresh. As the food historian Dr. Maricel Presilla explains, "There is red corn, black corn, purple corn, speckled corn, white corn, yellow corn."

Corn, the crop that was so plentiful it could feed a city, the product of knowledge shared across two continents, is central to the American food story. Along the Mississippi River and other areas where corn spread, there are mounds built by Native peoples to hold rituals. And across the river from St. Louis rose the great city of Cahokia, featuring large pyramids made out of earth and mud. By 1100 CE this city, fed by corn, housed some fifteen to twenty thousand people (the same as London at the time), with many more in the surrounding areas. When Europeans came to North America, they imagined the people were primitive, either savage or innocent, but certainly not capable of building cities. But that is only because—for reasons we do not yet understand—Cahokia had been abandoned by 1400, a century before any Europeans arrived.

The Native peoples of the Southwest learned to plant the "Three Sisters"—beans, squash, and corn—together. Beans helped to give the soil the nutrients corn needed. Corn supplied the tall stalks that the beans liked to climb, while squash leaves offered shade and squash plants prevented weeds from growing. Corn, beans, and squash together were tasty and healthy; where the Three Sisters flourished, the people could live. The Sisters all needed water, and the Native people developed thoughtful, well-planned irrigation systems, some of which are essentially still in use today. The Pueblo Indians (as the Spanish came to call them) grew the foods that suited their environment and shaped their environment to sustain their crops. "Pueblo" means "village," and the name shows that the Spanish recognized that the people lived in clusters of buildings. You can get a sense of these well-designed, linked homes, storage facilities, and spaces for rituals at sites such as Mesa Verde National Park in Colorado.

Starting around 900 CE and running to the 1300s, the Southwest grew hotter and drier, creating severe conditions that have only been matched recently in the era of climate change. The Pueblo were able to adapt to these climate threats until they faced both internal conflicts and powerful enemies, such as the Spanish. Then they were forced to abandon the sometimes three- and four-story homes they had created. When the Spanish arrived in the 1500s, they found some 278 areas, mainly along the Rio Grande, where Native peoples built their homes and grew their crops. The Spanish brought new crops, beliefs, and diseases.

By 1598 an expedition of Spaniards crossed the Rio Grande in search of gold and silver. Led by Juan de Oñate, the expedition included some seven thousand cattle, ten priests, four hundred men, and perhaps another one hundred women and children. After a clash in Acoma, in what is now New Mexico, Oñate initiated a massacre and a process of punishment and enslavement so severe, he was eventually recalled to Mexico and convicted of using excessive force. While the Spanish relied on native crops and knowledge to survive, they imposed new rules of ritual, faith, and living that aimed to erase the traditions of the Native people. The Pueblo fought back.

In 1680 a leader named Po'Pay, calling himself a prophet, rose among the Pueblo. Po'Pay spread word among the villages to gather arms and revolt—to shuck off the rites and rules of the Spanish and return to the old ways. Po'Pay claimed to have met three figures who shot fire out of their bodies. They told him to make a rope and tie knots in it, then send the fastest young men to carry it around to the many widely separated Native groups. Each knot stood for one day until their rebellion was to take place. Every group that agreed to join the fight was to send up a smoke signal.

Though the plot was given away to the Spanish and Po'Pay needed to act before he had planned to, the Pueblo did manage to work together and drive out the Spanish. Po'Pay then demanded that the Pueblo reject everything Spanish, even their livestock and crops, and return to their ancient beliefs, traditions, and foods. He promised that "they would harvest a great deal of maize (corn), many beans, a great abundance of cotton, calabashes and very large watermelons and cantaloupes; and that they could erect their houses and enjoy abundant health and leisure."

For twelve years the Pueblo managed to turn back and hold off the Spanish. Po'Pay's visions may have given new strength to the Pueblo, but the hot, dry climate did not change, which caused divisions among the Native peoples, and eventually Spanish firepower won. But the new Spanish rule aimed to ally with the Pueblo and to be more accepting of their ancient traditions. The culture of the Pueblo lands would be a mix of beliefs, crops, and ways of life drawing on Native, Mexican, and Spanish roots.

Amanda Palacios earned her master's degree at New Mexico State University studying anthropology, with a minor in food studies. Her family history captures this blending of Spanish and Mexican sources. Amanda focuses on the Lenten foods prepared and eaten in the Southwest United States, including Hatch, New Mexico—the chile capital of the United States. Lent, "Cuaresma" in Spanish, is a time of reflection and restraint for Catholics—such as Amanda's family—when they are encouraged to think about their lives and their actions toward others. As children, she and her sister would vow to avoid fighting and to skip sodas and sweets. The family would abstain from meat during Lent and would instead prepare special meatless foods linking them to family traditions. On Good Friday, the large extended family gathered, and everyone brought dishes such as chacales (dried corn soup with red chile puree), lentejas (green lentils), chicharros (split yellow peas with dried red chiles), nopalitos (cactus), pipián con tortitas de camarón (pipián sauce with patties made from pumpkin seeds and ground, dry shrimp), and capirotada (bread pudding).

The story of chacales extends back many generations. For

Amanda's great-grandmother, the process began during the corn harvest in August. She would attend a church service with her children, then go to the fields to gather corn. The ears that were not eaten that day were boiled, then tied together and left out to dry in the sun. Once the corncobs were completely dry, children would rub the dried cobs against one another to free the kernels. Adults would gather the piles and toss them from one bowl to another so that the wind carried away the "skins" covering each kernel. As Lent approached, Amanda's great-grandfather would bring a mallet and smash the kernels into pieces. Today Amanda can purchase the dried kernels, but the family still recalls the old ways. Corn kernels are boiled in water with garlic, along with onions, tomatoes, and chile colorado—a puree made from local chiles.

Amanda says the dried corn is "soft but hearty and has a very enjoyable texture. I would compare it to something like quinoa, but in the size of a corn kernel or cracked kernel. The dried corn has a subtle sweet corn flavor. Most of the taste comes from broth that has chile colorado puree, chopped onions, and chopped tomatoes. It is a light, clean soup. Chile colorado is spicy and gives a lot of flavor to the broth."

Hatch is the center of chile peppers for the whole country. Spaniards brought peppers from Mexico in the 1600s, and many varieties flourished. Amanda's mother remembers when they could choose from among chile puya, chile mirasol, chile guajillo, chile sancochado, and chile colorin. But early in the twentieth century, a brilliant local plant expert named Fabian Garcia— who has been called the father of the Mexican food industry in the United States—developed the Hatch chile, the chile that

Amanda's family and many others now use. Those chiles are still green when other plants are harvested, so many are left in the field when other plants are gathered. Some green chiles are picked to sell while other remain in the field. As the chiles mature, those acres of green turn red. The red chiles are picked just before the first frost, then dried the old-fashioned way in the sun or in ovens so they reach an even deeper brick-red color. Then the dried chiles are ready to be used. Chacales, served with pan blanco—which Amanda buys from local bakeries—is still a favorite during Lent. The Hatch chile—which links back to the Indigenous peoples of Mexico and is the modern creation of Fabian Garcia, a true food innovator—captures the ongoing and unfolding food history of the Southwest.

Southwestern food only begins the ongoing story of foods from Spanish-speaking lands. Ever since 1917, Puerto Ricans have been US citizens, and many immigrated to live and work in New York, Miami, and other parts of the country, bringing their foods with them. People from Spain opened restaurants in New York City early in the twentieth century. Cubans began fleeing during the Communist revolution when Fidel Castro came to power in 1959, and since 1965, Dominicans and other Caribbean islanders, as well as people from many Central and South American lands, have brought their distinctive ingredients and recipes to the United States. Portuguese-speaking Brazilians have filled the Ironbound district of Newark, New Jersey, and locations in other cities with their restaurants and stores. North, Central, and South America are, and long have been, more intermingled than many histories record.

Nachos

Nachos are the sort of food that people think of as age-old and traditional when in fact they were invented at a specific time and place and by a particular individual. This popular Tex-Mex snack (now sometimes expanded into a main course) consists of fried tortilla chips covered with melted cheese and any number of possible toppings: meat such as ground beef or chicken pieces; vegetables like green peppers, olives, tomatoes; chile peppers; and condiments like salsa, sour cream, and guacamole.

Nachos were first served in 1940 at the Victory Club restaurant in Piedras Negras, Mexico, just across the border from Eagle Pass, Texas, by Ignacio Anaya. A common diminutive nickname for "Ignacio" is "Nacho," and that is where the name comes from. According to locals in Piedras Negras, one night three women arrived at the Victory Club after the kitchen was already closed. They asked "Nacho" to make something for them, and he looked around to see what was in the kitchen. He cut up some tortillas into triangles, fried them, added cheese and pickled jalapeño peppers, and heated the dish in the oven—inventing the nacho.

Nachos were the signature dish of the Victory Club by 1950 and became popular in the US by 1960, although their real take-off was with the boom in the 1970s of the so-called Tex-Mex style, incorporating American and Mexican elements. The Dallas Cowboys began serving nachos during games in 1978, which led to the snack's big break. Howard Cosell was an outspoken sports announcer who held court as part of the *Monday Night Football* announcer team, along with former Dallas Cowboys quarterback Don Meredith and former New York Giants flanker Frank Gifford. Cosell was served a plate of nachos during one Cowboys game and began exclaiming about them on-air. Soon nachos were everywhere, and especially during games.

PART TWO

ENSLAVEMENT AND RACE, IMMIGRATION AND REACTION— TRANSFORMATIONS

Balbancha: New Orleans, Gumbo, and the "What-Ifs" of American History

Balbancha," the original name of the place that would become New Orleans, tells its own stories. Many Native peoples who lived along the Gulf of Mexico or the Mississippi (Algonquin for "Great River") met and traded near this crescent-shaped bend in the river. Each group had its own language as well as a common simplified version called "Mobilian" that allowed people from different groups to meet, trade, and understand one another. The Mobilian word for this meeting place was "balbancha," "place of foreign languages." The Choctaw version of the same word could also be seen as meaning "speaking nonsense, like an infant." (That sense of the word is just like the ancient Greek term that became our word "barbarian," which meant people whose language was so odd it sounded like "bar bar"—like baby talk—and no one could understand it.) This gathering place along the bend in the river was a spot where people who might otherwise be quite separate met. Modern New

Orleans is still a "balbancha"—with more new peoples and languages added into the mix.

New Orleans's food brings together native ingredients; Native American, African, and African American food knowledge; and European influences, including French, German, and French Canadian (Cajun). The dish that perfectly exemplifies this mixture—in more ways than one—is gumbo. Gumbo is a deeply flavored, dark, thick soup where surprising bites of meat, shellfish, and sausage bob up like secrets of the deep. And one of the first times that word was ever recorded was a magnificent feast that tells the whole fascinating story of New Orleans—and much of the United States west of the Mississippi.

There are at least three "what-ifs" leading up to this dinner, each of which could have totally transformed our history. All three turn on the tangled relations of France, Great Britain, Spain, and people living in North America.

First: When the French lost Canada to the British in the Seven Years' War (1756–1763), they hurried into an alliance with Spain. At least their new ally would block the British from expanding south, down the Mississippi. But when Spanish officials came to claim New Orleans, a band of citizens fought them off and then wrote to France asking to be returned to French rule. The letter suggested to several French high officials a grand scheme that would change the global balance of power. What they if turned all of Louisiana into a country of its own—protected by Spain and France and run by its own citizens—which might just inspire the restless thirteen colonies to demand the same and fight for independence from England? At a stroke the British would lose their colonies and any toehold in the continent. If this had happened, the middle of North America might have become a Franco-Spanish republic of its own *before* the American Revolution. But Spain was not pleased at the revolt in New Orleans and demanded that its leaders be tried and executed. This was only the beginning of the shuffle over Louisiana—and the grand celebration where gumbo was the star.

Second: Spain now ruled the port of New Orleans—and, in theory, all of the lands watered by the Mississippi and its tributaries. What was the extent of this land? How big was it, and who and what lived on it? While Native peoples had long-standing trade networks reaching far across the continent and so knew quite a lot about the land and those who lived on it, the Europeans were in the dark. They recognized that New Orleans could be an important port linking the products of North America with the lucrative sugar islands of the Caribbean and the important Spanish territories in Mexico and Peru. Beyond that there were question marks, legends, and fragmentary reports.

Enter André Michaux, a French botanist who was already an experienced traveler. He had gone to Persia in search of new plants and flowers and now was in America doing the same. In 1793 he convinced Thomas Jefferson to support an expedition he would lead across the continent. Meriwether Lewis made the same offer, but Jefferson thought the eighteen-year-old Lewis was too young and chose Michaux. This was a treacherous moment for the new United States. France's revolution in 1789 challenged all of royal Europe, and both Great Britain and Spain had declared war on France. The ideas of liberty, equality, and brotherhood that had been expressed in both America and France were also spreading through the sugar plantations in French and British colonial America in places such as Jamaica and Saint-Domingue (now called Haiti). This was inspiring to the enslaved people who harvested the sugarcane and to abolitionists, and deeply threatening to the defenders of enslavement. President Washington and his cabinet decided to remain neutral—not risking a new war so soon after the revolution. Spain refused to allow Michaux to cross into its territory, and Jefferson decided against sending him west.

Third: Napoleon eventually ended the age of revolutions and installed himself as emperor of France. Spain was not making much use of its territory in North America, so in exchange for it, Napoleon offered to give King Charles IV a bit of Northern Italy that the king wanted for his daughter. Napoleon had ambitious plans for Louisiana. As his chief diplomat put it, a Louisiana returned to French rule would be a "wall of brass" blocking either the United States or Great Britain from expanding across the continent. And it would bring real economic benefits: Louisiana would feed and provision Saint-Domingue, as that sugar-producing island was a source of great wealth for France. Louisiana mattered because the island's plantations were so important to France. But the Haitians defeated the armies of Great Britain and were now on the verge of turning back France. Thomas Paine, author of *Common Sense*, which had rallied Americans to fight in the revolution, suggested that the United States buy Louisiana and turn it into a haven for settlers, primarily Germans and some free African Americans. President Jefferson had other plans.

These alternate histories that never came to be—the Franco-Spanish republic, the French botanist exploring the west a decade before Lewis and Clark, the land for immigrants and the formerly enslaved—all show the tangle of forces operating in New Orleans, with France, Spain, Haiti, Great Britain, and the United States all competing, making and breaking alliances, as we will see in one grand celebratory dinner.

On December 8, 1803, the Spanish governor in New Orleans held a lavish dinner for the French. From the Spanish point of view, they controlled the city and the Louisiana Territory. But they were wrong. Pierre Clément de Laussat had arrived from France with word that due to Napoleon's secret swap, France was back in charge. On December 16, de Laussat's goal was to show French sovereignty by holding a dinner (if you can call a twelve-hour meal a dinner) that would be even more spectacular than the one he had attended eight days earlier, and he succeeded. Some of his throng of guests danced English, French, and Spanish quadrilles, galopades, and boleros while other gambled. Only 240 could be seated, so several hundred others ate while standing. The high point of the meal was the Louisiana treat of gumbo, and to make this event special, twenty-four different versions of the dish were prepared. De Laussat did not know that yet another treaty had also been concluded, selling France's rights to Louisiana to the United States. The meal that was meant to celebrate France's control of New Orleans turned out to be a fantastic ending to French rule. De Laussat's special dish lives on.

Gumbo takes us into the many layers of the New Orleans story and, more broadly, African American history. The name comes from the word for "okra" in several West African languages—for example, "okuru" in Igbo (a West African language from modern Nigeria), which became "gombo" in French. Okra is native to Africa, perhaps Egypt or Ethiopia, and spread across the continent, where it is often used to thicken stews. Okra came to the Americas not long after 1492, taking hold first in Caribbean cooking, and then to North America by the 1700s.

Free and enslaved Africans came to Louisiana early, both directly from Africa and via the Caribbean. From the beginning, Africans outnumbered Europeans in colonial Louisiana, and they had a vivid memory of their West African cultures and recipes. Africans of different nations shared their cooking techniques and developed a mixed or "creolized" African cooking, including dishes such as gumbo. With roots in the familiar West African rice-based dishes, gumbo was a cook's way of making do with whatever grains, proteins, and vegetables they had on hand.

What white people ate and thought of as "their" food was often prepared by Africans, who added their own ingredients, cooking styles, and tastes. And beyond dishes prepared for whites, African and African American cooking are only now being fully recognized for their roles in shaping so much of American food history. As Dr. Frederick Douglass Opie states about a great many foods and recipes, "too often white people have stolen the intellectual property of African Americans, taking credit for their discoveries."

Gumbo is a direct expression of African influence and more. The spicy stew can be thickened with okra but also with powdered sassafras, a plant (called "filé" in French) that the Europeans learned about from the native Choctaws. A third option, more directly French, is to combine fat and flour in a roux and use that along with—or instead of—okra or sassafras to bind a gumbo. The stew can feature many kinds of ingredients, including sausages, a contribution of Germans who first came to the city when it was controlled by the French.

De Laussat was especially proud that six of his twenty-four gumbos featured sea turtle. Sea turtles were highly prized by the original peoples of the Caribbean, by the enslaved people on sugar plantations, and by Europeans, who held great parties in which they shared giant turtles (up to nine hundred pounds) that had been sent from the islands to London or Philadelphia or other ports of the various empires. The arrival of a large turtle by ship would be announced in important port cities' newspapers, and some innkeeper or tavern owner would organize a party to serve it.

Versions of gumbo (although generally without turtle meat) are now available everywhere near New Orleans, from inexpensive local food shops to fancy restaurants. The thick, brown stew is made salty by generous slices of smoky andouille sausage, features any sort of poultry, meat, or shellfish, and is heated by a generous dose of cayenne. It is a kind of tasty "balbancha" gathered in a bowl.

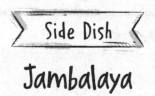

> Side Dish <

Jambalaya

A rice-and-meat combination, jambalaya is a classic dish of New Orleans and the surrounding countryside, the Cajun country of rural southern Louisiana. The Cajuns are descendants of French-speaking Canadians from the eastern coast and islands expelled in 1755 by the British in the wake of their conquest of French Canada. The territories along the Atlantic Ocean were called "Acadia," and the Acadians who came to French-ruled Louisiana came to be known by the related name "Cajuns." The Cajun version of jambalaya tends to be brown colored and flavored with meat gravy, while in New Orleans tomatoes give the dish a characteristic red color. Ham is the most common meat, but sausage is also often used, and now there are such things as shrimp or chicken jambalaya.

It's a bit of a mystery where the word "jambalaya" comes from, as well as what its origins are. At one time people speculated that the first part of the word comes from Spanish or French "jamón"/"jambon" (ham) and "yaya," the word for "rice" in certain West African languages. Jambalaya resembles the very popular tomato-rice dish of West Africa called jollof rice, but it is also reminiscent of Spanish paella. The word "jambalaya" appears in the early nineteenth century in Provence in Southern France, meaning a dish of rice with meat or vegetables. The Louisiana version incorporates ingredients and techniques from many cultures, and certainly tomatoes and hot peppers, which have American and African origins.

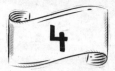

African and American: The Multiple Meanings of Fish Fries

1500s to Today

In Africa, Dr. Opie explains, long before the arrival of Europeans, people along the Senegal, Gambia, Niger, and Congo Rivers would use boats and nets to catch large quantities of fish—including local varieties of catfish. That is one starting point for the story of African American fish fries.

The date often used for the appearance of the first enslaved Africans in North America is 1619, but that is misleading. From their first expeditions to the New World in 1492, the Spanish had also brought Africans with them across the Atlantic to North and South America. Starting the European story in North America with the English is simply wrong, since the Spanish and French long preceded them. It also doesn't acknowledge the importance of the Southwest as a place where Europeans, Africans, and Natives met. Take the story of the astonishing Esteban de Dorantes (that is, Esteban was a Moroccan enslaved by Andrés Dorantes de Carranza). In 1527, Esteban and Andrés and two

others survived a shipwreck that left them off the coast of Texas. Over the next eight years they made their way walking across the entire Southwest until they eventually reached a Spanish settlement near the Gulf of California. Esteban often took the lead in meeting and learning from the many Native peoples they met.

Esteban was not the only African in the Americas. Spanish records from the 1500s list enslaved people in the Southwest from specific African locations, including West Africa and as far as Morocco to the north and Mozambique to the southeast. Recent DNA studies have shown that the first cattle brought to this region were African, and the earliest cattle ranchers were Africans, probably from West Africa, who were experienced herders.

If we switch from people to food and culture, even these early records begin too late. For as soon as Europeans began learning about the spices and crops of the Americas, they introduced and traded them in Africa. Cooks were mixing traditional African spices and foods with Asian ingredients and spices as well as new American flavors and ingredients before any of them were enslaved or sent across the ocean. Creative and experimental cooks quickly found tasty ways to turn American corn and cassava, chile peppers and peanuts into West African favorites. "African" food was already "African American" long before 1619.

When Africans arrived in the Americas, they brought their knowledge of food, seasoning, and cooking techniques with them. And then they added new knowledge and ingredients that they discovered or invented here. In some regions of Africa, palm oil or shea butter were used to fry catfish. It's unclear if Americans deep-fried their foods before 1492. But Africans certainly did. As Helen Mendes explained in *The African Heritage Cookbook*, "Contemporary Black Americans prepare fried fish in a manner very similar to that of their ancestors."

In parts of America where fish were plentiful, newly arrived Africans saw a familiar source of food. Fish were healthful, available, a link back to Africa, and free. Catfish, which were familiar and did not have many bones, were particularly popular.

You could find fried fish in cities as well as the countryside. Eliza McHatton-Ripley, a white woman who fled New Orleans during the Civil War, later recalled little stores "scattered about the purlieus and back streets, where white and colored laborers side by side ate fried fish or garlic stew." Elizabeth Henry, who cooked out of a cast-iron skillet on Garfield Street in New Orleans, became known as the queen of fish fries. In 1939 she was interviewed as part of a national project to capture the lives and stories of people throughout the country. The interviewer writes that "she could make a catfish melt in your mouth." Henry told him how she made her famous fish: She greased a frying pan and let the oil "get hot till it's almost smoking." She put her cornmeal "right next to my grease and take a fork and pass my fish through the cornmeal, and then I let my fish fry in the fryin' pan till it gets . . . a golden brown." As any fried catfish fan knows, you bite through the crispy corn crust to fish that is so delicious it is almost sweet.

After the Civil War, the fish fry on the Fourth of July became a regular event. Cooks filled large iron barrels with charcoal. Then deep cast-iron pans or skillets were placed on top to fry the fish a "rich golden brown," and it was served "piping hot." The author and anthropologist Zora Neale Hurston tells us that typically men caught and cleaned the fish and women fried them. She describes "happy houses" as those in which "hot grease began to pop" as they fried a batch of freshly caught catfish, perch, or trout. Fish fries were so popular that at a 1937 Mobile, Alabama, event, cooks fried "one thousand pounds of fish" for about a thousand guests.

West Africans used a locally grown peppery spice now known as "grains of paradise" to season their food and so arrived in the Americas with a taste for hot peppers and sauces. Over time they incorporated American plants into their hot sauces. Different peppers and liquids, such as the vinegar used in the popular Crystal Hot Sauce, create different flavors for hot sauces—which were always available to season fried fish. Hot sauce was so popular that a New Orleans cookbook reported African Americans lunching at oyster saloons carrying a "glass of Maunsel White (Tabasco sauce)" with them.

Starting in the early 1900s, approximately six million African Americans decided to leave the South. Faced with poverty, racism, violence, and very limited educational and job opportunities, they took the chance to move to expanding industrial cities such as Chicago, Detroit, Philadelphia, and New York. As people traveled in this Great Migration, they brought their foods and recipes with them. Soon women who were skilled cooks began serving familiar Southern foods in the cold North. The look, the smell, the taste of fried fish and other foods from back home made the new arrivals feel that these apartments and street corners belonged to them. In New York City, Lilly Harris Dean made her fortune selling home-cooked Southern specialties on the corner of 135th Street and Lenox Avenue in Harlem.

Grateful buyers in Northern cities could find familiar side dishes such as hush puppies, coleslaw, potato salad, corn bread, and collard greens with their fried fish. One more dish often served with fried fish has two origins—one of which can be found in "Yankee Doodle." A verse in that song, which was first sung by British soldiers making fun of the American revolutionaries, is "stuck a feather in his cap and called it macaroni." In the 1700s pastas from Italy, such as macaroni, were so new in Britain, they were chic, and the soldiers were saying the silly Americans were treating a feather as high fashion. The ladies in places like Virginia who aspired to be as fashionable as those in London recognized the value of the stylish dish and began to include macaroni in their meals. Most often those meals were cooked by enslaved African Americans. As pasta became more widely available, knowledge of how to use it spread through the Southern African American community. Then, in the twentieth century, as African Americans fled the violence and poverty of the South, they often lived in cities near Italian immigrants, who were fleeing the violence and poverty of Southern Italy. Macaroni and cheese was a dish common to both.

The North had its own forms of segregation, and especially during the Great Depression of the 1930s, times were tough. One way to help pay bills was by holding a "rent party." A person living in an apartment would announce a party, charge a small admission fee, and offer fried fish, chicken, and/or chitterlings—cleaned and fried small intestines—liquor, and live music to guests. The poet Langston Hughes remembered "Saturday night rent parties" which offered "good fried fish" as "more amusing than any night club." Those still living in the South during the Depression made use of the same strategies as their ancestors—fishing, growing vegetables, and keeping cows, hogs, or chickens so that they could feed themselves.

After World War II, African American-owned and operated restaurants continued to list on their menus fried fish served in various ways, with fish and grits and fish sandwiches the most popular. If you arrived at the Dew Drop Inn in Waynesboro, Virginia, on a Friday, you'd find fried fish along with grits and greens available all day long. Some African American restaurants offered fried fish or chicken every day by taking it off a dinner plate and instead serving it in a sandwich. Fried fish was changing from a traditional Southern dish to being a regular item a customer could eat anytime, anywhere.

During the Civil Rights Movement of the 1960s and the Black Power movement of the 1970s, food became a flash point. Some, such as the poet and playwright Amiri Baraka, pointed with pride to foods such as "hush puppies, fried fish, hoe cakes, biscuits, salt pork, dumplings, and gumbo" as African American foods that "came directly out of the Black Belt region of the South." As the African American cook and author Vertamae Smart-Grosvenor put it, "we cooked our way to freedom." That is, African Americans had fed the South—white and Black—while receiving little credit for their skill.

From the first, Africans in America had made use of whatever they found around them—such as catfish in the streams and rivers—adding just the right seasoning to create delicious dishes. Yet African American critics of the very foods listed by Baraka pointed out that fish were typically fried in unhealthful oils that contributed to heart disease. Elijah Muhammad, the leader of the Nation of Islam, for example, saw the traditional foods of the South as tools of enslavement—too fatty, too sweet, designed to keep African Americans sickly and weak. To these critics, African Americans needed more natural foods, fresh fruits and vegetables, not the fried foods of their parents and grandparents. He advocated for a healthier eating regimen for African Americans, full of fresh fruits and vegetables and legumes—particularly navy beans—and using natural sweeteners like honey for beverages and baking.

Amid these debates, several African American stars—including the boxer Muhammad Ali, the Gospel singer Mahalia Jackson, and the rhythm-and-blues powerhouse James Brown—started restaurant chains featuring their own versions of African American food. None of these ventures succeeded, but mass-market companies such as McDonald's soon realized that adding fried chicken and fried fish sandwiches to their burger menus was a smart idea.

Today, concerns over frying and health have led some African American restaurants to switch to grilled fish, and there are chains now (such as Hook & Reel) that offer fish and shellfish boiled along with potatoes, corn, and Louisiana spices. But whether prepared for large outdoor events, in restaurants, or at home, and fried, grilled, stewed, or boiled, fish are an African

American food tradition. As Bob Jeffries, author of *Soul Food Cook Book*, put it, "nothing could be more authentically soul than a supper of freshly caught fish, a fish stew, or an outdoor fish fry."

> Side Dish

Hush Puppies

Hush puppies are smallish balls of cornmeal batter deep-fried so that the outside is crisp while the inside stays soft. Starting around 1900, the term became popular in the South, and restaurants started serving hush puppies with fried shrimp or fish, fried chicken, or barbecue. Legend has it that hush puppies were invented to throw to dogs whining for food, especially at fish fries. This makes sense both because the fry cooks would have plenty of boiling oil and cornmeal left over from making the fish and because what else can the name mean or imply? It certainly sounds like a command: "Hush, puppy."

In fact, the term "hush puppy" and the fried cornmeal batter are both much older than the twentieth century, when they were first paired together. As far back as the eighteenth century, "hush puppy" was a slang term for a cover-up, as in, "They'll pretend to investigate the crime, but it will be all a hush puppy affair." And making cornmeal fritters or other deep-fried versions goes back equally far, a logical way of using a cheap and versatile ingredient.

An African American fish-restaurant owner named Romeo

Govan seems to have been not so much the inventor as the popularizer of what he called "red horse bread," "redhorse" being a kind of fish caught in rivers of southwestern South Carolina and eastern Georgia. How red horse bread became the hush puppy is a mystery, but the process can be followed through newspaper and magazine articles and the growth of fishing tourism in the early twentieth century.

> Side Dish

Potato Chips

Confusingly, "chips" are French fries in Britain, while potato chips are known there as "potato crisps." The original potato chip seems to have been invented in or around Saratoga Springs, north of Albany, New York, sometime just before the Civil War. Saratoga Springs was a luxurious resort, famous for its healing mineral springs and later the site of a horse racetrack. A number of claims have been made about who invented the potato chip (mostly African American chefs) and how the idea of slicing potatoes very thin so that they came out crispy was born. "Saratoga" potatoes had to be eaten quickly or else they would become mushy. For a while they were a delicacy, served with game birds like pheasant. Only in the 1930s were techniques developed to retain their texture through a manufacturing process, and they then became as popular a snack food as pretzels. Now, of course, they are even more popular and come in many flavors.

Eating English in America

1620s On

nglish settlers in the northeastern part of the New World, in the lands they named "New England," tried to reproduce the food of home. The newcomers expected to eat wheat bread, cake, meat from domestic animals (pigs, sheep, lambs), and familiar vegetables. They found a wide variety of potential new foods, many shared by the Native peoples, but not the familiar ones they preferred. The new lands offered game, new sorts of fruits and vegetables (pumpkins, squash, cranberries, lima beans), maple syrup, and lots of shellfish (clams, lobsters, scallops), but the settlers mistrusted this bounty, which they associated with the Native inhabitants.

Wheat did not flourish in the soil and climate of New England, but corn did. The new arrivals referred to this as "Indian corn" because in English usage "corn" meant grain. This Native corn, although made into a variety of products such as corn bread, pancakes, corn pudding, etc., was considered inferior to wheat.

To this day "corn" means "grain" in England, while our "corn" is "maize."

Hominy is a preparation of nixtamalized pounded corn kernels that was used especially for what was referred to as "hasty pudding," made with milk and water and cooked relatively quickly to resemble porridge rather than the traditional English boiled, solid pudding that required more time and effort. Corn could also be mixed with rye and baked into a bread known as "ryaninjun." These breads and puddings were eaten in many parts of British colonial America but were downplayed in descriptions of life in the colonies. Reliance on New World foods such as corn, clams, or cranberries rather than wheat and livestock made the colonists seems more "Native" and less like the "civilized" English.

Corn exported to Britain was used to feed livestock, not people. An English comic writer who went under the name of Ebenezer Cooke published a satire of colonial life in 1708 entitled "The Sot-Weed Factor" (i.e., the tobacco broker). The factor, a caricature of a crude, loud American, drinks hard apple cider and eats coarse food based in corn: hominy, corn pone, and cornmeal mush, flavored with molasses and bacon fat. The American colonists might have resented being described as rough-hewn rubes, but they agreed that the Native products were undesirable choices forced on them by necessity. One early chronicler wrote in 1654 that many settlers had found it hard to subsist on "Indian bread," yet they had no choice until cattle and plowed crops could be introduced. The Massachusetts Bay minister Cotton Mather (infamous for his role in the Salem witch trials) wrote with sadness that the poor depended on low-status food such as mussels, clams, and nuts. Even when praising the teeming fish and wildlife of New England, observers such as the Plymouth Colony governor William Bradford regarded game, fish, and Indian corn as barely acceptable, clearly inferior to the butter, beef, sugar, and wheat bread of England. The colonists longed for rich gravy sauces, roast mutton, pies, and bacon. Doubtlessly Bradford would have preferred wine or English ale to apple cider as well.

By the mid-1700s, New England had become prosperous, and its residents could afford refined sugar, spices, rum, and other luxuries. Tea, of course, was another product imported to America from Asia, and by the 1770s the 1.75 million North American colonists were drinking more cups of tea than the five to six million British. The Boston Tea Party is familiar as a step on the way to the Revolution, but the fact that so much tea was being sent to the colonies shows what a large market there was for imported luxury foods.

The mid-Atlantic region exported wheat to Europe, the West Indies, New England, and the South. New England sent rum, molasses, and fish to a similarly diverse set of destinations. All of these imports and exports were, in turn, tied to the trade of enslaved Africans to the sugar islands of the Caribbean. With the proceeds of economic expansion, Massachusetts bought wheat from colonies with better farmland such as Pennsylvania, and English-style white bread replaced ryaninjun and corn bread. By the mid-eighteenth century, New England meals were closer to those consumed in Britain than at any time before, ironic given that the Revolution was about to take place. Molasses, clams, pork, and ryaninjun had given way to sugar, beef, and cake.

The American Revolution began a gradual shift of New England food, and American food generally, away from English tastes. The new republic's wilderness and roughness were now seen as a healthy rebuke to tired and decadent Europe. The high mountains and seemingly endless forests of North America no longer suggested that nature ruled over people. Instead, American farmers were seen as strong, hardy pioneers building their own futures, free from the vise grip of ancient feudal laws, lords, and kings.

An early example of praise of America's simple culinary virtues is Joel Barlow's poem "The Hasty-Pudding," written in 1793. Oddly enough, "The Hasty-Pudding" opens with an evocation of the French Revolution, the liberties it brought, and the execution of the king. Barlow (who was living in France and involved in its politics) then turns to what the newly liberated common men of America eat, the simple breakfast of egalitarian America. Hasty pudding is healthful, simple, and democratic, but Barlow never says it is particularly delicious. Barlow's only reference to taste is the ominous observation that hunger encourages enjoyment (that is, starve yourself and anything tastes great). Ignoring flavor while praising convenience (it was, after all, a "hasty" dish to prepare) and healthfulness point to a strong thread in American eating that continues to the present day: the idea that eating simple, healthful foods (in a word, being on a diet) is far more important than flavor, taste, or pleasure.

The quest for a uniquely American culinary experience is

reflected in a cookbook entitled *American Cookery*, which appeared in 1796. Its author, Amelia Simmons, identified simply and mysteriously as "an American Orphan," was the first to claim to be describing the cuisine of the newly independent nation. As is often the case with cookbooks, *American Cookery* was actually less innovative than it claimed to be. Of its 192 recipes, fifty-seven were copied—today we would call it plagiarized—from British recipe books, sometimes with slight variations in wording or ingredients. A further eighty-one recipes have no identifiable source but are firmly within a tradition of British cuisine. Only twenty-three dishes do not come from Great Britain. These exceptions involve cornmeal, cranberries, pumpkin, and turkey, all identified with colonial New England. *American Cookery* is also the first place the Dutch-derived word "cookie" appears in print instead of the English term "biscuit."

Mary Randolph's *The Virginia Housewife* appeared in 1824 and—though Randolph herself did not admit this—points to another thread shaping and shifting North American cooking. By carefully reading the recipes, scholars have found the traces of African American cooks sharing their own knowledge, spices, and ingredients. This was true wherever enslaved people lived and worked, whether in the large plantations of the South or on small family farms where they cooked for both white and enslaved families or in the wealthy homes of the North.

Hasty Pudding

Here is the recipe for hasty pudding as written in Amelia Simmons's original cookbook. This is one of three recipes under the heading "A Nice Indian Pudding," and at a mere one and a half hours of cooking, the fastest. The second recipe requires baking for two and a half hours while the third has to be boiled for twelve hours. We are so accustomed to microwave time scales that this hardly seems hasty:

3 pints scalded milk, 7 spoons fine Indian meal, stir well together while hot, let stand till cooled; add 7 eggs, half pound raisins, 4 ounces butter, spice and sugar, and bake one and half [hours].

6

"You're Not Colored, Are You?"—Soda Fountains

1800s to Today

Today you can get flavored bubbly water in any vending machine, supermarket, or restaurant. There is a story behind those drinks—and their fancier cousins, such as milk shakes and ice-cream sodas—dating back thousands of years. In some natural springs, the rushing water captures minerals and carbon dioxide gas, which bubbles up at the surface. People have long considered those waters special—perhaps holy and certainly healthful. That made the springs destinations for wealthy travelers but did nothing for people who lived far away.

Sometime between thirteen thousand years ago, when humans began growing grains, and four thousand years ago, when the Sumerians wrote about this drink, brewers figured out how to make beer. Beer and fizzy spring water were the main options for drinks with bubbles until the 1600s and 1700s. (Other fermented drinks, such as kvass made from bread and kumiss from mare's milk, were and still are local favorites in parts of Russia and Central Asia.)

Born in England in 1614, Christopher Merret was trained as a doctor and was a founder of the "invisible college": a group of men who gathered to conduct experiments to find out the secrets of nature. This was a time when the categories of scientist, philosopher, author, botanist, experimenter, and even alchemist searching for magical secrets blurred together. In 1662, Merret figured out how to add bubbles to wine, in effect inventing champagne.

More than a century later, a fascinating Englishman named Joseph Priestley took the next step. Priestley was an open-minded minister who argued against enslavement and for the rights of all people. He was also an extraordinary scientist who studied electricity, shared ideas with Benjamin Franklin, and is credited with being the first to separate and identify oxygen. In 1767, Priestley tried a new experiment. He noticed that when beer was fermenting, the air above it seemed thick and still—we now know that he was seeing clouds of carbon dioxide. He placed a bowl of water over a vat where beer was brewing and added chalk and sulfuric acid to the fermenting mash. The additions created more carbon dioxide, which soon produced bubbles in the still water. He had invented what to this day is called "carbonation." When Priestley spoke out in support of the French Revolution, his home and church were burned down, and in 1791 he crossed the ocean to live out his days in Pennsylvania. By the early 1800s inventors in America followed up on Priestley's discovery, patenting devices to make fizzy water and then whole soda fountains.

In the 1850s A. T. Stewart, an Irish immigrant in New York City, came up with a big idea about shopping. At the time shopping for the home was done by women who had to go to different stores to buy thread, yarn, buttons, and cloth to make clothes, and to negotiate the price of each item with each seller. A shopping trip involved many skills, from knowing how to sew and budget to recognizing the the quirks and qualities of every merchant. Stewart created one store with many areas, or departments, and gave every item a fixed, "set" price. Then he began to hire women to make "ready-to-wear" clothing. Now a shopper could come to one location and wander among acres of items displayed on tables and racks. Those who had the money and the free time came to buy; those who could not afford the clothes could still browse and dream. Soon the new "department stores" added giant windows facing the street, in which passersby could browse the store's wares. Instead of a daylong test of a woman's skills, window-shopping and a visit to a department store were designed to be a kind of dream, an amusement park of items to consider and buy. What could be more refreshing in such a day of dazzling adventures than flavored bubbling water topped off with a scoop of ice cream?

Even as Stewart and soon others were creating department stores with soda fountains, another new kind of shop began to open. In 1751, Franklin helped to create the first hospital in America and then made sure the doctors were assisted by having an in-house store of medicines. His pharmacy was not like a modern chain drugstore, where anyone can walk in and pick up Band-Aids, toothpaste, and bottled aspirin. The trained expert behind the counter had to assemble and prepare the medicines patients needed. Pharmacists made use of books listing ingredients and instructions, some of which dated back to ancient Egypt and Greece and to medieval Muslim, Jewish, and Christian scholars, as well as discoveries made by Native peoples. In the 1800s these "compounding pharmacies" spread across America.

By the 1920s modern drugstores, which sold premade medicines, began to replace the old pharmacies. To attract new customers, the druggists added more items to buy in the front of the store and installed attractive soda fountains. Today many green drinks and smoothies made with nutrient-rich protein powders claim to be healthful—if they have no cane sugar or include vitamins or are made from berries with "antioxidant" properties. Soda jerks (people who prepared soda fountain drinks behind a soda fountain counter) made similar claims about the concoctions they whipped up a century ago. The drinks were based on "formulas," not recipes, and were thought of as health drinks and as alternatives to liquor. Since the pharmacists were known to understand how to mix ingredients to improve your health, people trusted their carbonated creations. The fact that they had lots of sugary, flavored syrups as well as ice cream was even better: good for you (according to the mistaken theories of the time) and pleasant tasting too.

In these Roaring Twenties one could find a soda fountain on the corner of just about every urban area across the country. Thirsty customers could be served an ice-cream soda in a tall glass graced with a spoon and a straw, and topped with a rainbow of sprinkles or a deep red maraschino cherry. A soda fountain was meant to provide a special experience: a sugary, fun, supposedly healthful treat served by eager-to-please staff in their crisp white uniforms.

An English visitor, Sir John Fraser, wrote about the wonders of the soda fountain: "On one side is a long white marble counter, and you sit on a high stool whilst white-clad young men spryly supply the thirsty mob. There is grape juice and loganberry juice, root beer, orangeade, coco-cola, cherry phosphate, lime-ade, mixtures of aerated water, crushed strawberries, chocolate sundaes, and ice cream of many colors and many flavors."

Soda fountains offered endless combinations of syrup and "aerated water" beyond those the visitor listed, including the black cow (Coca-Cola, chocolate syrup, cream, and ice cream), egg cream (whose New York version had neither eggs nor cream), lime rickey (lime, sugar, and seltzer), and sarsaparilla (similar to root beer). Milk shakes, "malteds," and ice-cream sodas, invented at soda fountains, became favorite treats. Soda jerks were a combination of bartender, pharmacist, and chef: they had to know how to whip up these combinations. Some drinks were designed to give a jolt of energy, a dash of buzz to the drinker. This was not just an advertising gimmick: soda makers put drugs such as caffeine and even cocaine (the original "coca" in Coca-Cola) into their creations. In 1929, just as the use of drugs in sodas was being regulated, a new drink came on the market: "Bib-Label Lithiated Lemon-Lime Soda." The drink *was* refreshing, in part because it included lithium salts, which are now prescribed to help patients with extreme mood swings. The salts remained in the drink, which eventually changed its name to 7UP, until 1948.

The era of sodas as medicinal formulas ended, but soda fountains had another key role to play in American history.

Precisely because the soda fountain was meant to be a place of pure sweetness and pleasure, it was exactly where contests over what is fair, legal, and just for all Americans took place.

In 1894, Abraham Cecil, an African American painter, walked into Hamer H. Green's pharmacy in Bloomington, Illinois, and ordered a "cherry phosphate"—a popular mix of cherry flavoring; phosphate, which provided a tang; and water. He was refused service, and a series of courts agreed that a soda fountain was not a public space—it was a private business. Black people were excluded from most white-owned soda fountains. Starting in 1877 a series of laws had allowed businesses, schools, and neighborhoods to exclude African Americans—reinforcing an image of "white" supremacy. The attitudes behind these laws were so extreme that even vending machines could be labeled "whites only," as if to allow the "wrong" thirsty person to buy a drink from a machine would violate the sacred rights of separation.

One way to trace the history of soda fountains in African American neighborhoods is through Thomforde's, which opened on 125th Street in the center of Harlem in 1903. William Thomforde was white, and for its first twenty years, Thomforde's was segregated and only served white patrons. Over time the restaurant changed policies, employed African Americans, and became a favorite destination in Harlem. The store's advertisements featuring its homemade candy were regularly run in the *Amsterdam News*, Harlem's newspaper. Malcolm X, who had worked as a soda jerk himself in Boston, enjoyed having desserts there. But when the employees insisted on joining a union for better pay in 1981, the Thomforde family instead chose to close it.

In many cities African Americans did not need to rely on white store owners. Black entrepreneurs opened stores and other businesses that met the needs of Black people, including soda fountains in African American neighborhoods. Starting in 1933, Sidney Barthwell operated a chain of thirteen pharmacies with soda fountains in them in Detroit. In 1936, Robert Shauter opened the first of three African American–owned pharmacies and soda fountains in Cleveland. The great jazz vibraphonist Lionel Hampton moved to Los Angeles as a teenager to attend UCLA during the day. At night he worked as a soda jerk, where he got to meet musical stars such as Count Basie. Standing behind the counter, Hampton used spoons as drumsticks to try out musical ideas. Though he broke too many glasses to keep the job, he soon landed his first gig as a drummer in a band.

Soda fountains—whether in Black or white neighborhoods—began to serve many functions. They were a place to meet friends that was not a bar, an appealing spot for dating couples, and a way for working women to eat during the day. Men had long been able to eat in bars and taverns, but it was considered improper for women to eat there. They could, though, have a sandwich at a lunch counter with a soda fountain. By 1941 the *Atlanta Daily World*, one of the first African American daily newspapers in the country, criticized women for eating a lunch consisting of "a couple of gobbles at a soda fountain" instead of what the paper considered to be a proper meal.

As appealing as the African American–owned and run soda fountains were, being excluded from white-owned businesses was an insult that African Americans refused to accept. As the *Baltimore Afro-American* reported in 1920, "white drugstores would rather go out of business than serve soda water or ice cream to colored patrons."

In April of 1943, led by Pauli Murray—a too-little-known pioneer in civil rights, women's rights, and gender fluidity—students at Howard University (a leading historically Black college) protested at the segregated Little Palace Cafeteria near campus. Their picketing, signs, and protests convinced the owner to open seats to all comers. The students began a second round of protests at Thompson's Cafeteria near the White House and succeeded there before the Howard administration told them to stop. The college leaders feared upsetting white politicians who determined how much support the college would get. Though the Howard campaign ended, the campaign against segregated lunch and soda counters was just getting started.

On July 7, 1948, African American civil rights pioneers tried once again to integrate soda fountains. The first case took place in Des Moines, Iowa, and the protestors won. Ten years later a teenager named Carol Parks Hahn took a seat at the fountain of the Dockum Drug Store in Wichita, Kansas, and ordered a Coke. "You're not colored, are you, dear?" the waitress asked. "Yes, I am," Carol replied, and from that point the waitress treated her as if she were not there. Carol and her friends (fellow high school students, such as Gayln Vesey) boycotted and picketed the store. "It was degrading, dehumanizing," Vesey recalls, and they took to the streets. By August, the store owner agreed to integrate his counter. This was the first teenage-led protest movement in the country. The Dockum stores were part of the national Rexall chain, and after the victory of the Wichita movement, Rexall integrated many of its lunch counters. Protests followed that same August at the Katz chain of drugstores in Oklahoma City, which finally agreed to let anyone sit, order, and sip at their fountains.

Two years later, on February 1, 1960, one of the most famous steps in the Civil Rights Movement took place at a similar location—the lunch counter of a Woolworth's department store in Greensboro, North Carolina. African American college students risked abuse and physical violence to "sit in" at the counter, which would serve only white people. The brutality of the white crowd was filmed. The protest movement spread and, by the end of March, reached fifty-five cities in thirteen states. That summer, lunch counters throughout the South started to integrate, and the Civil Rights Movement was fully launched.

Today coffee shop chains have replaced soda fountains as places to sit, meet, sip, and work. We linger on screens, meeting digitally even if we sit side by side, and make our own selections from a menu rather than seeing what a soda jerk can whip up for us. Flavored sodas and milk shakes come from bottles, cans, and the standard formulas of franchise restaurants. Our devices are our meeting place—and while we can order deliveries, our phones can't mix us a cherry phosphate.

Maraschino Cherries

Cherries come in many colors and kinds. Among the common American-grown varieties are red Bing; red-flecked, golden Rainier; and golden Royal Ann cherries. The marasca cherry grows in what is now Croatia, across the Adriatic Sea, east of Italy. Maraschino, a strong fruit brandy, is made with these cherries. In Europe fruit was often soaked in some kind of alcoholic beverage, both to give it a kick and some flavor and to preserve it in jars for months beyond the normal life span of fresh fruit. The process for preserving maraschino cherries was originally to marinate marasca cherries in maraschino liqueur.

These cherries were luxuries, expensive because of a limited supply of the marasca variety. They were used in pastries such as fruitcake, as an addition to ice cream, and, by the early twentieth century, featured in the newly fashionable cocktail. So, for example, a maraschino cherry is the typical garnish for a Manhattan cocktail.

For most of the past hundred or so years, however, the American maraschino cherry has been quite different: It is, first of all, not a marasca cherry but a more common type like Royal Ann. There is no alcohol content; instead, a brine (like what is used to make pickles) soaks the cherries before they are dyed bright red and packed in sugar syrup with almond flavoring. These cherries were mainstays of soda fountains. The perfect ice-cream sundae required a maraschino cherry on top of the final peak of whipped cream, and Coca-Cola could be flavored as a "cherry Coke" with the liquid from the maraschino cherry jar, garnished with a brilliantly red cherry. The same went for a cherry-lime rickey.

The Invisible Immigrants: German Cuisine
1700s to Today

The decorated Christmas tree, Santa Claus, the Easter Bunny, Easter eggs—not to speak of hot dogs, hamburgers, doughnuts, potato salad, light-colored lager beer (as opposed to dark, thick ale), and coffee cake—so many aspects of "American" life were German imports. Germans introduced ketchup, cucumber pickles, and the "Wiener schnitzel" that evolved into chicken-fried steak. Yet much of this German influence in food and culture is invisible. Almost always the nineteenth-century "immigration story" focuses on the Irish, the Italians, the Eastern European Jews. In fact, at the start of the twentieth century, the five million German Protestant, Catholic, and Jewish immigrants made up the largest single group of new Americans to have arrived in the previous century. The middle of the nation— the "German triangle" of Milwaukee, St. Louis, and Cincinnati— was one stronghold. German wheat farmers, who left Russia in the 1870s, brought their special skills and seeds to the Dakotas,

Nebraska, and Colorado, turning America into the wheat producer for the world. As it happens, the ships carrying wheat to Europe had lots of empty space on the return voyages—which is one key reason why it was possible for millions of poor Italians and Eastern European Jews to purchase cheap "steerage" space to move to America.

Germans had been coming to America since colonial days. Small Protestant religious sects seeking free space to practice their faith found homes in William Penn's tolerant Pennsylvania. Liberal and radical Germans whose efforts to change their society in the failed revolutions of 1848 fled to America, bringing their skills and idealism with them. Economic opportunity brought the largest swell of Germans in the 1880s, some 1.5 million people. By 1894 there were eight hundred German-language newspapers and magazines across the land.

Generations of Germans brought their foods, drinks, music, and culture with them. The German-born cartoonist Thomas Nast's drawings of the jolly "Sinterklaas" (which were published in newspapers from 1863 through 1881) set the new image of Santa Claus. By the 1850s German beer gardens and basement beer halls ("Rathskeller") became popular. The beer gardens were among the first restaurants of a type that would now be called "family-friendly." Even though by definition a beer garden was a place to drink alcohol, its atmosphere was safe and picnic-like rather than gloomy and threatening, as taverns could be. Americans wondered at the presence of children at establishments where drink flowed but on the whole were favorably impressed. German restaurants popularized smoked sausages, ground meat patties, lager beer, and various types of cakes and snacks (like pretzels) that soon lost their particular links to Germany. Popular eating places, such as Manhattan's Luchow's on 14th Street and Chicago's The Berghoff on West Adams Street (which still exists), were destinations for locals, celebrities, and tourists.

And then came the big change.

World War I began in 1914, and America was determined not to join in. Indeed, Americans were not sure which side they favored. Many Irish Catholic Americans were more inclined to see England—which refused to grant Ireland independence—as an enemy than Germany. Jewish Americans who had fled tsarist Russia were unlikely to want to fight by its side against Germany. German Americans—who read German papers, flocked to concert halls to listen to German music (from the majestic orchestral music of Beethoven to the enthralling operas of Mozart and epics of Wagner) were aligned with their homeland. But when America entered the war in 1917, the entire tone of the country shifted. A massive propaganda campaign defined Germans as "Huns"—brutal monsters. And to be associated at all with the German enemy was to be un-American.

Sauerkraut was renamed "liberty cabbage." Hamburgers became "liberty steaks." Frankfurters changed into "hot dogs." German shepherds transposed into "Alsatian wolf dogs." Esteemed concert halls now stressed Italian operas. Classical music was no longer a chance for German audiences to be proud of the composers of their homeland—it was a universal language. Pretzels were banned from saloons. And the rise of the movement to ban alcohol, especially on Sundays, was in part a judgment and criticism of the German beer gardens.

German Americans became Americans. Many had been here for several generations, spoke perfect English, and wanted their children to do so as well. They were eager to assimilate—and to avoid being seen as alien, different, suspect. By World War II, this process was already in place. German neighborhoods, such as Yorkville in Upper Manhattan, still featured specialty sausages and pastry shops. But those were small enclaves. The overwhelming majority of Americans of German heritage were not eager to stress their background. And their foods had been absorbed into the general American diet.

> Side Dish

Pretzels

Although the pretzel may have been invented somewhere else in Europe, the German immigrants to Pennsylvania brought over the twisted, soft variety. It was considered an ideal accompaniment to beer. Barkeepers did not want to be bothered serving elaborate meals but needed to provide drinkers with snacks to keep them drinking (preferably salty snacks to maintain their thirst). The hard, thin pretzel was invented later, in the mid- to late-nineteenth century, and these became a typical snack not only for bars but everywhere—in school lunches, for example, and on airplanes.

The anti-German sentiment that resulted from World War I and Prohibition, which closed bars and was supposed to get rid of alcoholic drinks, decreased pretzel sales and threatened the popularity of this by-now-classic snack, but it survived to become something independent of beer drinking, like its close cousin the potato chip (see Side Dish in Chapter 4).

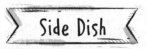

> Side Dish <

Irish and Jewish: the Immigrants Who Did Not Transform American Food

Approximately 4.5 million Irish came to America between 1820 and 1930, and 2.75 million Jews. Yet neither group has left a lasting influence on American food. As we near mid-March and St. Patrick's Day, many supermarkets and restaurants will feature corned beef and cabbage and various cookies dyed green. Certainly there are Irish-style taverns, bars, and pubs throughout the country. But no version of traditional Irish fare has gained broad popularity. In part that is because the majority of Irish immigrants were poor and had an extremely limited diet both at home and when they first came here.

Jewish influence is evident from bagel shops, which can be found everywhere, though what is called a "bagel" today has almost nothing to do with the hard, slightly bitter items Jews brought with them from Eastern Europe. Visitors to New York City at one time sought out Jewish "delis" to taste overstuffed pastrami or Reuben sandwiches, but again, this was a novelty, not a lasting contribution to national cuisine. Now, on late nights, the remaining delis host fashion-conscious young people sporting "delicore" styles. Because observant Jews obeyed dietary laws not shared by many others, Jewish immigrant cooking evolved to serve its own communities and only slowly adapted to broader "American" tastes—but by that time many second- and third-generation Jews were eagerly eating Chinese, Italian, and African American foods themselves.

8

Scientific Nutrition: "Plain Food Is Quite Good Enough for Me" (and Healthier Too)

1893 to Present

In 1893, Chicago hosted the World's Columbian Exposition—marking four hundred years since Europeans and Africans landed in the Americas. When the United States had celebrated its own one-hundred-year anniversary seventeen years earlier in Philadelphia, the star of the show was a massive steam engine that supplied electricity to all the exhibits. The Chicago fair was bigger and better—a larger engine, an entire "White City" constructed to show off how beautiful new buildings could be, as well as what was called a "Midway Plaisance"—a wide walkway lined on both sides with endless amusements. In the six months of the fair, more than twenty-seven million visitors came to sample its pleasures. At the Chicago exposition, the United States demonstrated its power and glory—to itself and the world. The fair also helped to shape our entire food history—in several different, almost opposite, ways.

As we have seen, some Americans had long treasured the

foods of their lands—salmon climbing the Celilo Falls, the Three Sisters and nixtamalized corn feeding the Southwest, fresh catfish caught in the South, the balbancha of ingredients in a gumbo. But the exposition was not there to honor the many peoples and foods of the country. One exhibit did feature Nancy Green, a woman who had been enslaved prior to the Civil War, dressed as a pre-war enslaved cook, making pancakes with Aunt Jemima's pancake mix. The demonstration was extremely popular—but it did the opposite of honoring the cooking skills and contributions of African Americans. It used the figure of an enslaved "mammy" to sell a new product. (The company kept the name and image of the smiling, turbaned African American woman as its symbol for more than a century, until 2021; it is now called the "Pearl Milling Company Original Pancake & Waffle Mix.")

All those visitors strolling, hungry, eager for treats, made for great opportunities for smart food sellers. Historians dispute whether Cracker Jack debuted there, but Juicy Fruit gum and shredded wheat did, as did Vienna Beef, a popular Chicago hot dog. H. J. Heinz was not happy that the selling spot for his ketchups and pickles was on the second floor, so he spread golden signs all over the first floor promising a prize for anyone who mounted the stairs. His "pickle pin" drew crowds and made his company an enduring success. The fair was an ideal place to promote and advertise new, easy, appealing, and sweet treats. That was one way it influenced American tastes. It was also the home of a model kitchen, demonstrating to visitors what cooking in the home "ought" to be.

The Rumford Kitchen was set up to educate the "intelligent, thinking citizen" in proper and economical nutrition. "The fate of nations," announced one of the kitchen's mottos, "depends on how they are fed." How should a nation eat? A second motto quoted the respected Civil War veteran, author, and future Supreme Court justice Oliver Wendell Holmes Jr.: "Plain food is quite good enough for me."

We are still living with both sides of the fair—snacks, sweets, and industrial foods, and also ever-new rules (sometimes followed, sometimes ignored) about dieting, food, health, and which vitamins and supplements to take.

Back in colonial days, elite Americans had prized what they saw as the foods of England, especially wheat and beef. It is perhaps revealing that even at this celebration of the Americas, the model kitchen was named after Benjamin Thompson, an American scientist who was a Loyalist during the Revolution, fought for Great Britain, moved there, was knighted by George III, and was named the "imperial count of Rumford" (hence the name of the kitchen) in Bavaria. Rumford did study foods and cooking and gave money to create the Rumford Chair of Physics at Harvard, but using a Loyalist turned aristocrat as a model for Americans was telling. The association of correct cooking with Great Britain went beyond one name.

In 1863, *Mrs. Beeton's Cookery Book*—a British publication that became a bible of cooking in the entire English-speaking world—confidently asserted that wheat was the healthiest grain, followed, in order, by rye, barley, and oats, with rice and corn least valuable. Wheat, she insisted, was necessary for "civilized people." Linking wheat and beef to a ranking of races and people was much in the air. "Those races who have partaken of animal food are the most vigorous, most moral, and most intellectual of races," wrote an English scientist. Since England and the rising United States seemed to be destined to rule the world, this idea was quite convincing.

On January 24, 1872, word was released that the emperor of Japan—where killing animals had been prohibited since 1687— was now regularly eating beef, and the government created a company to promote beef and dairy products. Back in the United States, the American Federation of Labor argued for excluding Chinese workers from the country because they ate rice. "You cannot work a man who must have beef and bread . . . alongside of a man who can live on rice." According to the AFL the hearty, strong beef-eaters would be "forced down" to the feed of the deprived and inferior rice eaters. This connection of prejudiced racial theories and fanciful food science had begun earlier in the century.

In the 1830s people who saw themselves as food reformers urged Americans to change their diet radically, demanding that the nation turn away from self-indulgence in food and drink and eat with careful and proper restraint. Food was something to be tamed rather than enjoyed. Science seemed to require this brand of careful eating. In 1847 the German chemist Justus von Liebig showed that foods were not just what you saw on the surface: they contained proteins, fats, carbohydrates, and minerals. No one knew exactly what these things did or which mattered in what way. But experts insisted that some foods were better for you or answered specific needs. The taste and look of a dish were less important than what it did for your health.

After the Civil War those who studied this new science of

nutrition saw the human body as a kind of machine that must be fed the most efficient fuel. These nutritionists believed in reform, but as a choice between "good" and "bad" foods a person made for themselves, as if the social and economic conditions had nothing to do with poor diet. Poverty, illness, disease (they claimed) were products of weakness, self-indulgence, and the wrong foods. In Southern Italy a terrible disease called pellagra had been all too common for more than a century. In the twentieth century it began appearing in children in the American South. According to the food reformers, the Italians were sickened not by the fact that they were poor and so ate "badly" but by their too spicy, too oily, too complicated, too often vegetable-based foods. Vegetables and fruits were considered empty and unnecessary foods compared to hearty, protein-rich beef. Where cuts of beef were not available, people were urged to drink beef broth. Garlic, critics claimed, was turning Italian peasants into alcoholics. Poor whites and African Americans in the South ate corn and pork, not "healthy" wheat and beef.

Most of these supposedly science-based food-reform ideas were wrong. Fruits and vegetables are, in fact, necessary. Milk and meat are not perfect nutritional foods that guarantee health. All these facts and pseudo facts were used to make an argument that personal as well as national strength and character depended on properly supervised and rather boringly plain nutrition. Very similar claims are made today by people who criticize poor people for drinking (cheap) sugary beverages or eating (cheap) fatty meats—rather than making sure that healthier options are available and affordable for all.

Southern Italians and Americans living in the Southern states suffered from poverty—they lived on a limited, filling diet. The corn of the American South was not nixtamalized, so it did not provide the niacin people needed. Bad food was not making people poor. Poverty was forcing people to eat whatever could fill their stomachs. But that was not how the scientific nutritionists saw it. If Italians were to become healthy Americans, they needed to change their diets. A social worker in Columbus, Ohio, wrote critically about an Italian family that they were "still eating spaghetti, not yet assimilated."

The most radical and long-lasting food-reform idea was that taste in food did not matter. Ignorant people are guided by what tastes good, the food reformers insisted. One leading nutritionist imagined with horror a poor woman saying, "I'd rather eat what I'd rather. I don't want to eat what's good for me." The food reformers devoted themselves to combating this attitude. Their argument was a two-part view that is still with us: (1) I like this, so it's probably bad for me, and (2) eat this—you may not like the taste, but so what? It's good for you. Despite the efforts of such social workers, food reformers, and nutritionists, Italian immigrants continued to cook rich, complex meals. As they earned more money in America they added a greater variety of fruits, vegetables, and meats. But if immigrants were uncooperative, there was a different potential audience ready to listen to the apparent science of cooking and eating.

The Rumford Kitchen in Chicago was not designed to convert Italian immigrants or the Southern poor. The reformers faced a dilemma—they believed that some races were superior to others, as revealed by the foods they ate. Could the races be "improved" by changing their foods? If so, how important was race? If not, how important was food? They decided that Italians, Russians, African Americans, and Jews were hopeless, while Germans, English, some Catholics, and Protestants could be helped. The way to do that was by reforming and educating middle-class people—always eager for self-improvement—who would set the example for others. The Rumford Kitchen's intended audience was middle-class housewives, who were being instructed in how to take on the supreme task of providing for a healthy family. The wife, insisted Harriet Beecher Stowe (the abolitionist author of *Uncle Tom's Cabin*) and her sister Catharine Beecher, was the "chief minister" of the "family state," and it was her job to make the home into the earthly echo of "the heavenly kingdom." The Rumford Kitchen could show the way through "the application of the principles of chemistry to the science of cooking."

Foods thought to be healthy and favored by superior races included beef, the newly invented breakfast cereal, store-bought bread, and milk. Food was to be healthy and bland, not over-stimulating: baked beans, oatmeal, codfish—the supposed menu of New England pioneers. The plainer the better. According to a wealthy scientific amateur and patron named Horace Fletcher, every bite must be chewed at least one hundred times, until there was absolutely no damaging flavor left. Taste stood in the way of good digestion, and "Fletcherizing," as this unpleasant practice was called, promised mental calm and clarity, not just physical health.

In the early twentieth century these middle-class Americans began to have a new idea of what a healthy body should be. Rather than showing that you were jolly and enjoyed life, as in the Thomas Nast Santa Claus drawings, being full-figured was a sign of weakness or self-indulgence. A healthy body was slim and athletic. The right foods, the proper diet, self-restraint, would help you gain and keep that figure.

Starting in 1912 scientists made a series of new discoveries about foods—they contained more or less of crucial yet invisible ingredients: vitamins. It's true that we do need vitamins. The disease of scurvy that afflicted sailors on ships was a result of a lack of vitamin C. Pellagra came from living on corn that could not release niacin. But once advocates identified invisible ingredients that made all the difference in health, food could be entirely disconnected from pleasure or taste. A bland white bread filled with vitamins could be called "Wonder Bread," and mothers were assured that it could "build strong bodies twelve ways." As America entered the twentieth century, ideas of science, food, race, and health intertwined, and some are still with us today.

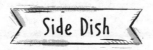

> Side Dish <

Breakfast Cereals

Most people in other countries have no idea what cold cereal is and would be surprised to learn that many Americans consider it appropriate for breakfast. In some places, leftovers from yesterday's meals are eaten at breakfast, so there is nothing very distinct about the meal. In many European countries, a small amount of bread and jam or a pastry or hot cereal (such as oatmeal) might be consumed. For many people, including Americans, breakfast is the most predictable and reassuringly repetitious meal of the day. While you don't want to have the same thing for lunch or dinner every day, you might be perfectly happy to eat the same cold cereal with milk and maybe fruit every morning.

Americans started eating cold cereal in the late-nineteenth century because it was presented as healthful, especially for children. Up until then most Americans who had enough to eat in the first place had morning meals of eggs, bacon, sausages, toast, and the like. To the food reformers we have described, this did not seem frugal or a healthy way to start the day.

Medical entrepreneurs like William Keith Kellogg and C. W. Post came up with the idea of toasting wheat, rice, bran, and other grain products and serving them as health foods. Kellogg ran a kind of spa (called, at the time, a sanatorium), which had both sick people and those who, while not sick, wanted to improve their health or learn tips on "wellness." At Battle Creek, Michigan, Kellogg and his brother ran a resort hotel on the principles of the Seventh-Day Adventist Church—a vegetarian diet being among the teachings of this group. Kellogg presented his diet ideas not just as leading to good health but as a kind of moral reform as well. Breakfast cereal would make you a better person, give you a psychological edge and more energy than the sluggishness-inducing indulgence of the conventional breakfast. Snappy brand names, tinkering with the flavor (for example, adding sugar), and relentless advertising (especially about how these toasted corn-flakes, puffed rice, or shredded wheat were good for you), along with the belief that milk was a kind of miracle food, transformed the American breakfast. By the first years of the twentieth century, breakfast came to be based on this newly invented food. For most of the twentieth century, cereal was regarded as the healthiest breakfast food. It took nearly that whole century for vegetarianism to become more widely accepted, as it is today (see Chapter 12).

Red Sauce Rebellion: Italian Restaurants Change America's Food Story

1910s to Today

I n the early years of the twentieth century you might run into the children, grandchildren, nieces, and nephews of the women who created the Rumford Kitchen dining out. These young people, many of them graduates of the most elite Ivy League universities and the parallel Seven Sisters colleges for women, would not be eating oatmeal and beef or carefully chewing their bites one hundred times. Instead, you would be likely to find them at a place like Bertolotti's Restaurant at 85 West 3rd Street (a building in which Edgar Allan Poe had lived while he revised "The Raven" and wrote "The Cask of Amontillado") in Manhattan's Greenwich Village. Bertolotti's was run by Angelo and his wife, whom everyone knew as "Mamma." At lunch she offered a rich minestrone (a thick vegetable-and-pasta soup full of the kinds of flavorful ingredients the nutritionists had warned against), along with Italian bread and red wine (another sign of moral failure, according to food and moral reformers) for fifteen cents—tip included (approximately five dollars today). The warm familial environment, the large portions of tasty food, and the cheap red wine were perfect for a generation of young people rebelling against the cold, rigid world of their parents with its social conformity, its sharp splits in the roles of men and women, and its meant-to-be-boring foods.

Take John Reed, a Harvard graduate who lived blocks away at 42 Washington Square. As he wrote:

> Yet we are free who live in Washington Square,
> We dare to think as Uptown wouldn't dare,
> Blazing our nights with arguments uproarious;
> What care we for a dull old world censorious
> When each is sure he'll fashion something glorious?

And those impassioned debates were fueled by exotic wine and spaghetti. There was a kind of perfect irony in this twist in the American food story: young people rejecting a "British" view of their country to embrace dishes based on tomatoes—yet another ingredient first grown in the New World, then spread around the globe, only to return in the "red sauces" of Italian restaurants.

The Greenwich Village young people, referred to at the time as "Bohemians," included reporters and writers such as Reed, along with poets; painters; dancers; Eugene O'Neill and other playwrights; labor organizers such as Emma Goldman; and women (and men) fighting for women to get the right to vote, to work under safe conditions, and, following Margaret Sanger, to have access to contraception. There was Grace Nail Johnson, whose father was a key real estate agent opening Harlem to African Americans and whose husband, James Weldon Johnson, was an author, diplomat, executive secretary of the NAACP, and co-creator with his brother, John Rosamond, of "Lift Every Voice and Sing," which became known as the African American national anthem. Both gay (so-called long-haired) men and lesbian (so-called short-haired) women were public and visible—which was extremely unusual at the time. There were also pretenders, playing at being radical to be part of the fun.

Similar, smaller gathering spots for young artists and rebels could be found in Chicago and San Francisco, as well as in large cities in Europe. Indeed, all these centers of rebellion looked to Paris as their North Star. Paris was where the new abstract art was being created by Pablo Picasso and Georges Braque, the new dance by the Ballets Russes and especially the electrifying dancer Vaslav Nijinsky, new music by Igor Stravinsky, new poetry, new theater, new posters, new politics—the new, everywhere. Greenwich Village was a touch of Paris in America, except that the food was Italian.

French cuisine had long been available in America—for the elite. As in Europe, French food was considered the height of cooking, the very best, and so restaurants that catered to the wealthy—such as Delmonico's in New York—filled their menus with complicated dishes that required the steady hand of a chef trained in French cooking. But the Paris the radicals looked to was not the home of dishes whose sauces required lengthy and precise presentation. They were as eager to declare their break with their parents in what and how they ate as they were in their poems and plays, strikes, and protest marches. The meals at Bertolotti's were just right. They fit the budget of artists who were never sure where their money would come from, and they were a visible way to reject the rules of the previous generation. The radicals were inventing a new kind of eating in America: You didn't just eat what your family had always eaten or—if you could afford it—French specialties. You might try another culture's foods—and experiences. You experimented.

Gonfarone's was another Italian restaurant in the Village, on the corner of MacDougal and 8th Streets. The owners offered more than good food: they hired a waiter who juggled as he served, a cook who acted out a scene from an opera—rushing out of the kitchen holding a knife as if to attack a rival—busboys who offered their harmonica solos. The idea was that an Italian meal should be fun and excessive in a harmless way: a three-ring circus of plates arriving and being cleared, grinning waiters, musical sounds where too much was just right. This sort of adventure in eating soon appealed to people who were out to have a good time, not to change society.

In 1906 an Italian immigrant named Girolamo Leone and his wife, Luisa, opened a restaurant in New York—not in the Village, but still linked to the arts. Leone's was next door to the Metropolitan Opera, then on 39th Street and Broadway. The great Italian star of the day was the tenor Enrico Caruso, whose celebrity status rivaled that of later rock stars. He was said to have been such a fan of Luisa's cooking that he encouraged her to open a restaurant. Attending the opera was one way

RED SAUCE REBELLION

the richest and most prominent New Yorkers established their standing and their wealth, but it was also a passion among poor Italian immigrants—as popular as any music or sports event might be today. Leone's was there for the singers, the artists, the cheap-seat fans. The opening-night menu offered everything from appetizers and soup to pasta and chicken, salad, cheese, and spumoni (see Side Dish on p. 92), as well as wine for fifty cents (about seventeen dollars today). Soon other Italian places, such as Asti on 12th Street, just on the edge of the Village, hired waiters who could sing. At set times they would burst into song, tackling famous operatic arias and inviting customers to join in.

In the 1950s Italian food made its biggest leap. First in cities, then as malls spread across the suburbs, one particular cheap street food from Naples in Southern Italy won over Americans: pizza. Men had been able to buy elaborate meals in bars since the 1800s, working women grabbed daytime meals at lunch counters, and those who had time and money could lunch in restaurants offering salads and "light" fare such as egg-salad sandwiches. Now the many young families of the postwar baby boom could find a quick, hot snack everywhere that was a treat for children and filling enough for an adult. Pizza offered a hint of being "real Italian," but each buyer could decide whether to add garlic, oregano, sausage, hot pepper—or could even create their own versions, stretching from extra cheese to pineapple. As pizza became a national favorite, spaghetti and meatballs went from being exotic to so familiar, the dish was sold in super-markets in cans, frozen, and as separate ingredients so one could prepare the meal at home.

The growing crowd of Italian-food lovers filled the restaurants, which needed to expand. Leone's began with twenty tables in 1906; by the 1950s it held 1,200. In 1914 the restaurant had moved away from the Metropolitan Opera into the growing theater district. Luisa Leone worried that they would lose customers. But Victor Herbert, a famous composer of light operas (focusing on romantic, fun plots and pleasant melodies, not hyper-intense dramas and tragedies), told her, "Mother, for you and your wonderful cooking, I'd follow you to the ends of the earth." The theater district was the right spot for Leone's (which changed its name to "Mamma Leone's" after Luisa died in 1944). As the customers shifted from Italians to Bohemians and then to anyone wanting a good time, the menus became more standard. Mamma Leone's became a tourist destination in New York, serving up to four thousand people a day. Everyone from the First Lady Eleanor Roosevelt to the war hero (and future president) Dwight D. Eisenhower sang its praises. The restaurant was so popular that in 1959 the family finally sold it for millions to a corporation—which only closed it thirty-five years later because the Manhattan real estate it occupied (and owned) was so valuable they could not resist selling it. The restaurant was torn down to make space for a much larger building.

In sixty years Italian food had gone from being the symbol of everything scientific nutrition rejected to being so popular that waves of tourists couldn't wait to try it out, and pizza swept the nation. Other cuisines followed. Eating as a form of exploring another culture was taking hold.

Side Dish

Pizza

More than two thousand years ago, in Pompeii, guests were offered a round flat bread topped with pomegranate seeds and spices. Perhaps this is a distant ancestor of modern pizza. Pizza's recent history begins in Naples, where it was a street food. Originally it was a type of sweet, flat cake with almonds, but by the nineteenth century, the word was applied to a flatbread with some simple toppings such as lard (a form of pig fat sometimes used in place of butter), garlic, and/or tomato sauce. Pizza was associated with the common or poor people of Naples, although King Umberto of Italy and his wife, Margherita, sampled pizza when they visited the city in 1889. According to a popular story, because the queen particularly liked one made with mozzarella cheese, it was named "pizza Margherita" after her.

Just as there are competing claims for who invented the potato chip, credit for the first pizzeria in the United States is in dispute. In New York City, Lombardi's seems to be the oldest, but even before it opened as a store around 1897 and started serving pizza a few years later, there were Neapolitan immigrants selling pizza to their homesick neighbors.

Pizza became popular in Italian urban neighborhoods during the first decades of the twentieth century. Key to its expansion into an American favorite was that it became more elaborate with more options. Instead of just cheese and tomato sauce, sausage or pepperoni could be added, anchovies as well, and finally almost anything—pineapple, which was first popular in Hawaii, or mashed potatoes, popular in New Haven, Connecticut. Different cities and regions developed their own styles, from the deep-dish pizza of Chicago to the thin, burned-crust pizza of New Haven.

After the end of World War II, pizza became popular all over the United States. Pizza was a tempting fast food because you could see and smell it as you stepped up to the counter, it could have different toppings, and it could be eaten by groups sharing a pie or as a single slice. One of the largest and most successful chains, Pizza Hut, got its start in the early 1960s in Wichita, Kansas, a place with few Italians. Pizza is a profitable fast food not just because it is popular but because the ingredients are inexpensive and the dough can be made in advance or frozen (although this affects the quality of the pie).

In the last decades of the twentieth century, Domino's perfected a system of delivering pizzas that basically dispensed with actual stores. Here too the product quality might not be the same as pizza ordered in a restaurant, but the convenience of delivery is irresistible.

> Side Dish <

Spumoni

Spumoni is a type of gelato (like ice cream but with somewhat less fat). "Spumo" means "foam," and while this dessert is not literally foamy, it has a slightly whipped texture in comparison to the traditional hard ice cream, and so it can be molded into many shapes. It is multicolored and often has small bits of candied fruit and nuts embedded in it or between layers.

In Italy the classic spumoni flavors were cherry, pistachio, and either vanilla or chocolate. The most popular American variation was what is called "Neapolitan," three bars or layers made with the more familiar flavors of vanilla, chocolate, and strawberry and without the nuts and fruit (you could add your own nuts, chocolate, or caramel sauce, etc.). Most Italian immigrants to the US came from Southern Italy, especially Naples, and many foods like spumoni, common throughout Southern Italy, were identified with the city.

PART THREE

FRANCHISE AND FRACTURE—HAVE IT WHOSE WAY?

10

Howard Johnson's: Franchising 28 Flavors and Fried Clams

1920s to 1990s

In the 1960s a family that was driving on any major highway in the United States would be likely to see a familiar orange roof over a roadside restaurant. Everyone in the car would probably want to stop at that Howard Johnson's (which was affectionately called "HoJo's"), where they would find grilled cheese and burgers, steaks and fried clams—and twenty-eight flavors of ice cream. Today there is not a single Howard Johnson's restaurant left (the last holdout closed in 2022). The rise and fall of those restaurants tells many stories about this country in the twentieth century.

Howard Deering Johnson grew up in the Boston suburb of Quincy, Massachusetts. When he was sixteen (in 1913), he dropped out of school to work for his father's cigar business. By 1925 the company was failing, and he tried his luck running a local soda fountain. Johnson soon realized that his most popular product was ice cream. Tinkering with that success, he figured out how to make ice cream that was smoother, creamier, and richer than the local competition. In four years, he developed twenty-eight flavors—from vanilla and chocolate to maple walnut, burgundy cherry, and peanut brittle. The ice cream was so popular it caused traffic jams as families lined up to buy it. Soon Johnson opened ice-cream stands at nearby beach resorts.

In the 1920s Americans were rushing to buy cars—some twenty-six million were sold in that decade—to drive on the four hundred thousand miles of new, paved roads. Cars made it easy for families to go on trips together, but where would they eat? The existing highway eateries offered cheap meals for truckers or traveling salesmen, men who would probably never come back to those places. In 1935 one food reporter found only 167 decent roadside restaurants in the whole country. Johnson decided to solve that problem by creating a chain of roadside restaurants. He would "serve the finest food on the American highways at reasonable prices."

From the 1920s to the 1940s, being told that your food was identical to what others were eating was reassuring. For example, White Castle, which first opened in Wichita, Kansas, in 1921, helped to change the hamburger from a ballpark novelty to a mealtime regular. In 1932 the company reassured customers that "when you sit at a White Castle, remember that you are one of several thousands, you are sitting on the same kind of stool; you are being served on the same kind of counter. . . . The hamburger you eat is prepared in exactly the same way over a gas flame of the same intensity." Howard Deering Johnson extended the same ideas to roadside eating. A HoJo's was no greasy spoon with who knew what standards of cleanliness. It was the best of both worlds: a safely predictable chain but with lots of choice—all those flavors of ice cream. Johnson had a great plan until the big-spending 1920s came to a screeching halt.

The stock market crash of 1929 and the ensuing Great Depression drastically slowed car sales, road building, and even the growth of families. Then in 1941 America entered World War II, sending men and women off to war. Fewer and fewer Americans were taking family road trips. This could have put an end to Johnson's grand scheme. Just the opposite. The difficult times made it impossible for Johnson to borrow enough money to build new restaurants, so he turned to another option: franchising. That is, he would create a model of a Howard Johnson's in every detail, from what the restaurant must look like down to the hedges and parking lot, to creating all the food and freezing it in a central location, to detailing exactly how many glasses of water should be filled before lunch and ready for customers. A local businessperson would pay Johnson for the right to use the name, the menu, and the food. The owner was putting up the money, betting that the Johnson name would bring in customers. That is exactly how today's food chains work. McDonald's, for example, provides the brand, the look, the food. Each local owner pays for and manages the restaurant.

Once the war ended, many Americans rushed to start families. In 1956, Congress agreed to spend twenty-six billion dollars to create forty-one thousand miles of interstate highways criss-crossing the country. Now, instead of a day trip to a local beach, families took long drives to vacation spots. And they needed to eat at a place they could trust with treats for everyone in the car, from a toddler and teen to a parent. Along every stretch of highway there was a HoJo's to answer their needs. By the 1960s Howard Johnson's served meals to more Americans than anyone else except the US Army.

Johnson's menu was relatively standard, but with some quirks and twists: hamburgers were called "hamburg steak"; hot dogs were "frankforts." Children could order jelly sandwiches, but peanut butter was reserved for pairing with bacon in sandwiches. Broiled chicken and sirloin steak were listed to please adults. Johnson had grown up in Massachusetts, and he made some New England dishes, such as Boston baked beans with brown bread, a regular on his menus. An especially New England keynote was fried clams—a regional specialty that went national as the Howard Johnson's chain expanded. People old enough to remember Howard Johnson's when it ruled the highways have especially fond memories of those crunchy, plump fried clams.

By the 1960s, when restaurants like Mamma Leone's were booming, versions of "Italian spaghetti" and "Italian-style ravioli" were added to the menu as well as a few Chinese American-style dishes, like a chop suey roll. The sixties also brought the same civil rights challenges to HoJo's that it did to soda fountains nationwide. In 1962 the "Freedom Highways" project set out to desegregate restaurants along the highways in Maryland, Virginia, North Carolina, and Florida—a first step toward challenging racist practices in the Deep South. Some HoJo's quickly agreed; others—especially those owned by local franchisers—resisted. The following year North Carolina made integration in chain establishments mandatory, and by 1965 that became national law. HoJo's followed the law, but it did not take a stand in the civil rights struggle.

McDonald's and soon others realized that families didn't need waitstaff, didn't need table service, didn't need twenty-eight choices of ice cream or a menu that (at one time) required the central kitchen to create more than four hundred dishes. One quick, cheap, tasty item—a grilled hamburger—served in a clean restaurant with child-appealing treats was enough. Howard Johnson's had trouble changing its image to suit a new generation. Fast-food places were new, appealing, and popular with trend-setting teens and young families. HoJo's seemed like spots frozen in the 1950s and associated with an earlier, more boring, and bland time. A change of leadership in the company led to valuing price over quality, and so there was even less reason to pick the fading old restaurants over the exciting new ones. HoJo's proved that the franchise model could fill highways with identical restaurants. Modern franchises have learned that you can do the same thing cheaper, faster, better and land on every mall and highway off-ramp.

Side Dish

Food Trucks

As far back as the Middle Ages, people in Europe sold prepared food such as baked pies from carts or portable stands at markets or events such as town festivals or parades. The diner began as a horse-drawn or, later, motorized vehicle that showed up to sell food at the gates of factories, which were often located in neighborhoods with few services. Workers who had night shifts also depended on the vendors conveniently parked near the factory gates. A special kind of mobile food began in the 1920s when Harry Burt (following the lead of Christian Nelson, the inventor of the Eskimo Pie) coated his ice cream with chocolate, put it on a stick to make it easier to eat, and began carrying around his Good Humor bars in trucks equipped with freezers and bells (to signal that they were coming).

In 1974, Raul Martinez created the first taco truck, in Los Angeles. By 2008 food trucks with an ever-wider variety of food were becoming a familiar sight on both coasts and in college towns. The bad economic time the nation was experiencing made inexpensive yet tasty and convenient food all the more popular. The trucks are now regulated in many cities—to make sure they are clean and the offerings are safe to eat. Food trucks can now be found everywhere, expanding the choices for hungry people eager for a favorite dish or to try something new.

> Side Dish <

The Automat

In 1902 the Horn & Hardart company in Philadelphia created what would be one of the most memorable restaurant chains: the

Automat. What people remember of the now-extinct Automats is the wall of small glass windows with handles from which a customer could, upon payment of a few nickels or a quarter, remove a ready-made slice of pie, a salad, or another small item. There was a regular cafeteria that served hot food, but the windows were, especially for kids, the real magic. Each time a piece of cake or a bowl of Jell-O was removed, the revolving tray at the bottom of the opening turned to bring forward another cake slice or an identical bowl of cubed Jell-O. For children, dropping a few nickels into a slot and pulling out the pie slice and then seeing it replaced was magical. You had the feeling of being inside a modern but entertaining machine.

The Automats were inexpensive, so much so that legend has it that during the Great Depression of the 1930s, when unemployment hit record levels, poor people put (free) ketchup into a cup, added (free) hot water, and had themselves a kind of tomato soup without having to pay anything.

Shopping through Chinese American History

1850s to 1965 to Today

I n the twenty-first century the number of Chinese restaurants in the United States far outpaces the total number of McDonald's, Burger Kings, and KFCs combined. This is a truly remarkable turnaround since—as we saw in Chapter 8—nineteenth-century Chinese "rice eaters" were vilified and worse. The story of Chinese American food is also the story of waves of prejudice and progress in this nation.

The first group of Chinese immigrants to the US were laborers who came to find work during the California gold rush of the 1850s. There were about four thousand Chinese in California in 1850, and just two years later some twenty thousand. In the 1860s Chinese who were here already and others who were recruited to come played a key role in building the transcontinental railroad. Often the Chinese crews did the most difficult and dangerous work, blasting through mountains and constructing high bridges for the tracks to cross. Yet out of prejudice by the other crews, as well as reluctance by the Chinese, they do not appear in the famous photographs celebrating the golden spike that joined railroad lines across the country.

By the 1870s an economic depression in the country fed anti-Asian prejudice, and the Chinese were subjected to violence and ever more restrictive laws. In 1882 the Chinese Exclusion Act banned all immigration from China. The Chinese, though, built communities in cities such as San Francisco and New York, where they opened markets and restaurants. Most of these entrepreneurs were men from Southern China, many from the region near the ports and the city of Amoy (now Xiamen). The foods and recipes they were used to at home were based on a style of cooking known as Cantonese cuisine, which uses a wide range of ingredients and a set of sauces based on soy and a balance of sweet and sour. It does not use intensely hot spices.

The Chinese who first came to America could not exactly reproduce the foods from their homelands—few of them were trained cooks, and they had to work with whatever ingredients and spices they could find here to recreate what they ate at home. Still, the American version of Cantonese cooking became—and still is—the kind of Chinese cooking most frequently found here. In China itself Cantonese is only one of eight main cooking styles—just as, for example, traditional New England foods are different from those of New Orleans. If all the visitors from China only went to New England, they might never know about gumbo. A version of Cantonese cooking in America came to stand for all Chinese food for a time.

By the 1880s, the restaurants opened by Chinese Americans

created dishes and treats that were not exactly Chinese and pleased other Americans, such as chop suey, chow mein, and egg rolls. Chop suey, for example, was probably originally "chao zasui"—a traditional Chinese mixture of animal innards quickly stir-fried at high heat with vegetables, mushrooms, bean sprouts, and spices. Chop suey was fast, tasty, and cheap—which appealed to the same kinds of early twentieth-century eaters experimenting with spaghetti at Italian restaurants. Over time, recognizing the tastes of American eaters, pork was used in place of ingredients such as gizzards and intestines, and a thick brown gravy replaced the quick, high-heat, stir-fried taste. Chao zasui had become chop suey.

In the early twentieth century, Chinese American restaurants were popular but still seen as exotic—which could seem both exciting and edgy. One striking fact that observers noted was that both whites and African Americans ate at these restaurants— easily relaxing and laughing side by side, if not together. This kind of mixing was extremely unusual, if not forbidden, in nearly every other place that served food. Chinese restaurants also tended to stay open late and so became gathering spots for single men and women who would have felt out of place dining alone during regular hours. Eating Chinese food allowed customers to step outside the "normal" mainstream while eating dishes that had become comfortably familiar.

The fact that some young people living in large cities were eager to reject the prejudices—and foods—of their elders did not mean the country as a whole agreed. While some radical causes—such as women getting the right to vote—succeeded, others did not. By 1924 the kind of bias and racism that had excluded Chinese immigrants in 1882 swept through Congress. New laws sought to "restore" the United States to its supposedly white, Protestant, and Northern European roots by strictly limiting immigration from Southern Italy and Eastern Europe while banning altogether any Asians, Africans, and South Americans. America so severely shut its borders that it would admit only the smallest fraction of Jews and others, such as the Roma, who were fleeing in the 1930s and 1940s from Hitler's death camps. For Chinese Americans who were already here, this was a period of assimilating and not standing out. Because Chinese people were banned from coming here, very few were arriving, bringing their languages, foods, and recipes with them. The Chinese already here built American lives, cut off from the influences of their parents' homelands.

From the 1930s on, Chinese restaurants began to expand past cheap, popular, Americanized dishes such as chop suey and added egg foo young (omelets with vegetables), lobster and duck preparations, and wontons—in soups, fried, or barbecued. Restaurants expanded, had more lavish decorations, and some added "Polynesian" dishes and cocktails. Chinese American food—built on a Cantonese base but adjusted to American tastes—had a secure place as a familiar choice, cheaper and more limited in some spots, more expansive and costly in others.

A legendary but plausible story is that one important addition to the fans of Chinese food came in the 1940s and 1950s in cities with large Jewish populations. As the children and grandchildren of the first immigrants assimilated, many were not strict about following dietary laws. When Christmas closed most restaurants, these Jewish families would head to Chinatowns—where the restaurants were open—agreeing not to notice that the dumplings contained pork (forbidden to observant Jews) or that shrimp (also forbidden) might be featured in a dish.

In some ways the 1960s were an echo of the early 1900s. Once again a generation of educated young people in high school and college rejected the beliefs of their parents and grandparents. They marched against the war in Vietnam and for civil rights and racial integration, for women's rights, for reproductive rights, and to change immigration laws.

On October 3, 1965, seated beneath the Statue of Liberty, President Lyndon Johnson signed a new bill, finally reopening the doors to the United States. The creators of the bill were ready to admit people from everywhere, though they did not anticipate quite how wide the doors would open. For, given the opportunity, people came from all over the world: from China, Korea, and Japan, from Central America, South America, and the Caribbean, from the Middle East and Polynesia. And for the first time, voluntary immigrants came from African nations, including Nigeria, Ghana, and Somalia. They all needed to eat, to shop, to cook, and to build businesses. Before the new law, markets selling Chinese products could only be found in the "Chinatowns" of cities. With the more open door, Chinese Americans branched out from the cities to the suburbs. Visiting an Asian market in a suburb is one way to walk through Chinese American history.

David Zheng was born in China and has studied and produced his own films on cooking in China. He takes us shopping—showing how Chinese Americans select and use ingredients grown here that allow them to adapt traditional recipes to current conditions. Shopping is not just making a list and picking up packed foods; it involves knowing how to identify the best products, building relationships with particular stores and sellers, and having the ability to adjust a menu plan to what looks best that day.

The experience of stepping into an Asian food store for the first time: the pungent combination of fish and a wide variety of vegetables overwhelm all the senses, and shoppers are surrounded by colorful packages with labels in a wide range of languages. For many immigrants, entering an Asian market is a brief and sudden step back to their home countries, every aisle carrying familiar smells and packaging that can be traced back to a treasured moment. Maybe a package of rice crackers was an essential item for every field trip, and here a shopper can once again experience a taste that they thought only belonged to their memories. For the Asian Americans born in the US, an Asian market is a portal back to their ancestral home, where they can put together the dishes that their parents used to make. In the 1950s to 1960s imported foods such as bamboo shoots, Chinese sausages, and preserved duck eggs became popular. These imported foods still occupy a section of Asian markets, but there is also a large area of Asian foods produced in the United States. These might include soy sauce made in California and tofu made in New Jersey. There's also a network of farmers who are stocking the produce of these markets. (The Academy Award–winning film *Minari* is a story that centers on a family of Korean American farmers.)

When going through the aisles, Asians and Asian Americans are also reminded of the grocery shopping skills passed down through generations. They remember their parents banging the watermelons to test the freshness, opening the egg containers to check that none of them are cracked, and never ever buying the first item on the shelf. In the soy sauce aisle David sees choices, each of which suggests a dish or a use: light soy, dark soy that is viscous and is used to color a dish, shoyu for sushi, low-sodium soy for dipping, and then he notices a brand he grew up with and saw daily in his parents' home. Buying the brand is a link, a connection to his family, his childhood. He loved reading Michelle Zauner's memoir, *Crying in H Mart*, because her experience as a Korean American was so similar to his in an Asian store. She noticed "a group of young Chinese students, alone without family at schools in America. They have banded together to take the bus forty-five minutes outside the city, into the suburbs of a foreign country, for soup dumplings." Looking at the many different Asians in the market, she realized that "we are all here for the same reason. We're all searching for a piece of home, or a piece of ourselves."

In the seafood section many kinds of fish and shellfish are displayed on top of banks of ice—like a hillside with diamonds of ice instead of grass, and fish instead of bushes or trees. Here is one of the few places where David can buy shrimp with their heads on. The shrimp heads add flavor to the shrimp and make wonderful soup stock. But David thinks that Chinese people don't like wasting food and prefer to see the animal they are going to eat—a whole fish with its head, a whole shrimp—not a piece pre-carved to disguise its origin.

Asian markets also carry the weight of the history of Chinese immigration to the United States. To this day Asian supermarkets stock mainly Cantonese vegetables. David is from Northeastern China, and his cuisine and ingredients differ greatly from Southern China. When browsing through the vegetable aisle, he is confronted with vegetables that he has no idea how to cook even though they are undeniably Chinese. Gai lan (Chinese broccoli), for example, used to be the must-have dish in every Cantonese restaurant in the United States but was not a vegetable David would have bought himself for home cooking. And that is just China. Many Asian supermarkets devote separate aisles to a variety of Asian nations and food preferences: one has Japanese products, the next, items from India, then Thailand, Malaysia, the Philippines, and more. You can see this variety easily when you reach the section piled high with bags of rice.

Rice is the most essential ingredient in a Chinese pantry. Rice goes with everything, including steaks. You can have congee—a rice porridge mixed with meat or vegetables—for breakfast, rice with lunch, fried rice for dinner, and sticky rice as part of a dessert. When the Dragon Boat Festival comes on the fifth day of the fifth month, people in China make zongzi—sticky rice that is wrapped in bamboo and then steamed. In the south, they like their zongzi sweet. In the north, where David is from, they prefer meat in their zongzi. As a northeasterner, David likes starchy short-grain rice. He cannot stand the dry long-grain rice they have in Southern China. Asian markets are very aware of the highly specific demands shoppers have for their favorite type of rice. That is why they fill an entire section with rice choices.

Although David has noticed that Chinese immigrants mainly stick with Chinese meals, second-generation Chinese Americans have somewhat assimilated to a more typically "American" diet. But Chinese festivals often remind them of these roots. The full moon shines bright in the sky, and it's the fifteenth day of the eighth month in the Chinese lunar calendar. Unlike Chinese New Year, Mid-Autumn or Mooncake Festival has gone unnoticed for many who aren't so familiar with Chinese traditions. Although it is the second-most-important Chinese festival, big celebrations are unusual here in the US. It has become a festival marked by Asian Americans buying mooncakes and remembering to look at the moon. This day is also a subtle reminder to call your parents and wish them a happy Mooncake Festival.

Like many holidays in the US, Chinese holidays are strongly associated with food. Even though it's called the "Mid-Autumn Festival" in Chinese, we now consider it the "Mooncake Festival."

Many American cities and businesses have now embraced the Mooncake Festival. It helps that a delicious pastry is at the center of this festival. Traditionally these are pastries made in beautiful, elaborate molds and stuffed with a dense filling. Mooncakes now come in such a variety of flavors and shapes that many are unrecognizable to the older generations. Parents might prefer the mooncakes with nuts and egg yolks, whereas the younger generation might choose the fruity flavors or green tea and even ice-cream mooncakes. It seems like any pastry in a mooncake mold can be deemed a mooncake.

General Tso's Chicken

This dish of crisp, fried chicken pieces in a sweet and spicy sauce is probably the single most popular "Chinese" dish in America. Often it is served with broccoli and dusted with sesame seeds. Who was General Tso, and what does he have to do with a food preparation unknown in China? The first part is easier to answer than the second: General Zuo Zongtang (1812–1885) was from the province of Hunan and had a successful career as a military leader and regional governor. He was involved in suppressing the Taiping Rebellion (1850–1864) against the Chinese emperor. This is maybe the bloodiest civil war in history.

Hunan is famous for its spicy food, but the general was not known for either his cooking skills or gourmet enthusiasm. In fact, Peng Chang-kuei (1919–2016), who was born in Hunan, invented the dish in Taiwan in the 1950s. After the Communist forces completed the takeover of mainland China in 1949, refugees and government officials settled on the island of Taiwan, which called itself the legitimate "Republic of China." For Chef Peng, naming his dish after a famous compatriot made sense. He did not choose the most famous child of Hunan, since Mao Tse-tung was the architect of the Communist victory that caused Chef Peng and others to flee from mainland China.

The original General Tso's chicken was not as sweet or crispy as the American version. The real innovation, due to Chinese restaurant chefs in 1970s New York, was to feature cubes of skinless chicken breasts with a crispy coating, topped with a sauce that is sweet as well as hot. American Chinese food generally is much sweeter than what is found in China, and American tastes include a preference for boneless and skinless meat and the combination of sweet and spicy (barbecue sauce is another example).

The 1970s saw President Nixon's visit to China, which first opened direct contact and quickly improved relations between the two countries. Its gastronomic spin-off was an interest in more authentic and varied Chinese food, especially from provinces with hot, spicy cuisine, such as Szechwan (now spelled "Sichuan") and Hunan. General Tso's chicken became popularized as part of the chile-peppery cuisine of Hunan. No one asked about whether this was authentic to the province, and even now, when it is pretty widely known that it isn't, the taste is so beloved that people don't much care that no one eats it in China.

12
First Foods Again: Twenty-First-Century Foods

In the 1970s a new kind of food market began to appear in cities. There had long been stands all along country roads where farmers would sell vegetables and fruit grown right there or honey from local hives. At this time some growers came to two realizations—they were not selling very much at home, and there were potential buyers in cities. They would not need to sell to the supermarket chains, which demanded huge amounts of identical, durable products. Instead, farmer's markets started up on specific days in centers such as New York City and San Francisco, where local growers could bring in and sell small quantities of ripe, tasty fruits and vegetables. The markets were wildly successful. Seasonal produce was soon joined by locally caught fish and locally harvested oysters and clams. Flower stands, vendors of duck, quail, and chicken eggs—literally butchers, bakers, and candlestick makers—all came. Many Americans have more access to what are now called "first foods"—fresh, seasonal, and from nearby farms—than they have had in a century.

The spread of local and "natural" foods was encouraged by another development of the 1970s. At that time large super-market chains were as dominant as fast-food franchises. While the stores might have had different names, acres of aisles were filled with similar products grown on mammoth farms or manu-factured in huge factories. Yet in many regions—near Boston; in Austin, Texas; in Los Angeles; in Maryland—small stores started up that went in a different direction. They featured what they called "natural" or "organic" foods, often locally grown fruits and vegetables. (The term "natural" means nothing artificial has been added, so a carrot or an apple may be natural, but that does not mean it is "organic." "Organic" broadly means foods grown without harmful chemical fertilizers or pesticides.) The stores had odd names, such as "Bread and Circuses" (the stores sold wooden toys along with food), "Mrs. Gooch's" (started by a fourth-grade teacher with that name), and "Bread of Life." By the 1980s, one by one, these local stores were bought by Whole Foods Market and made into a new kind of chain, which itself was bought by Amazon in 2017.

Here we are today—with farmer's markets still spreading, Whole Foods available both in stores and online, and even the old chain supermarkets featuring locally grown and organic produce along with the names and pictures of the family that raised those eggs or that crop. Ethical and environmental con-cerns about eating meat are being expressed daily with ever more force. The shift to food that is closer to the soil, that has not been processed or filled with artificial ingredients, has spread to restaurants. Indeed, one of the most well-known and expensive restaurants in America—Eleven Madison Park in New York City—has changed to an all-vegetarian menu. In 2022 the prestigious James Beard prize for the very best new restaurant in the country was awarded to Owamni, a restaurant in Minneapolis led by Native American chef Sean Sherman, which uses only ingredients that existed here before 1492.

We are no longer in the days when restaurants advertised selling identical, industrial products. And yet chains and franchises are, if anything, more dominant than ever. A chain will give us burgers or veggie burgers, local food or food from the other side of the world separately or side by side. Commercials, like those for burgers and pizzas mentioned at the beginning of this book, come at us all day long, urging us to buy ever larger portions of unhealthy food. Yet we are also constantly reminded to avoid potentially harmful foods and to improve our diets—not just to be healthier but as a sign of being better people.

In the dairy section of a supermarket you are likely to find whole cow's milk, two-percent milk, one-percent, and lactose-free versions of each; oat milk, soy milk, almond milk, cashew milk, coconut milk, sesame seed milk, and yogurts with varying fat and sugar contents (with or without probiotics, "Greek" strained or unstrained) made out of each of these "milks"; there is salted and unsalted butter, richer European butters, and organic butters, as well as reduced fat, olive oil, and nondairy butters. The dairy case is a kind of Google search for each shopper.

Yet beneath this seemingly open choice, the old structures

remain. Just as poverty, not pasta, led to pellagra in Italian immigrants, access to healthy foods depends on having money and living near stores carrying these products. Choice for some is absence for others. Many people with limited incomes live in what are called "food deserts," areas where it is difficult to buy affordable, healthy food because there are few or no grocery stores or supermarkets. The available "convenience" stores are loaded with cheap but often unhealthy snacks.

And then there is cost: one study showed that you have to spend about $1.50 more per person each day for fresh fruits, vegetables, and fish than for industrially made foods. For families "living from paycheck to paycheck," that extra may often be too much. Approximately 12 percent of Americans, or forty-one million people, live in these "food deserts." More than half of the children in this country live with uncertainty about what or whether they will be able to eat each day. As we saw in Chapter 8, it is easy to blame people with limited incomes for making unhealthy food choices, but often those selections are not "choices," they are necessities.

You may recognize current challenges and conflicts in the stories of prior generations that fought for civil rights, for women's rights, for integration, for immigration, and against prejudice. And today there are the additional challenges of climate change, of pandemics, of gun violence. How will those struggles intersect with how we shop, eat, and cook?

Animal rights advocates and those concerned that maintaining large herds of cows to produce beef has damaging environmental consequences urge us to at least reduce our meat consumption or, better yet, to become vegans. How plausible is that for the wide variety of Americans of different backgrounds, economics, and favorite foods?

We eat today as we are today. We have endless choices and deep structural problems and conflicts. That makes sense: as we have tried to show in this book, every bite we take reflects the wider world in which we live. Each smell and touch and taste can be the beginning of a journey into family history and memory. Recipes written down or shared orally can lead us into the larger national and international connections that define how we live our lives. When we look at the many ways Americans eat and have eaten, we break down the myths of our past and celebrate our variety. And today we can look beyond the advertisements that bombard us to sell foods produced in bulk to please some carefully researched "average" customer and can savor the many different spices and sweets, meals and snacks, that mean so much to each of us. Every bite is a story—waiting to be told.

> Side Dish <

Hand Foods

The fact that John Montagu, the fourth earl of Sandwich, liked having sliced meat and bread brought to him (whether while working or gambling is disputed) gave us the name of what once was the assumed easy lunchtime centerpiece. If not for him we might have called them "trenchers," for the medieval European stale round breads that served as plates and then could be eaten after absorbing sauces and drippings all meal long.

Since the advent of pizza, though, sandwiches have ever more rivals for snacks or meals that combine a protein—meat, fish, eggs, cheese—with vegetables, sauces, or flavorings and some form of grain or bread to hold everything together. Many of these have long existed in cultures around the world, and now are available here. For example, there are Arabic or Israeli falafel; Bengali fuchka; Caribbean roti; Chinese bao; Colombian or Venezuelan arepas; Greek gyros; Indian kathi rolls; Italian panini; Mexican or Tex-Mex tacos, burritos, and tortas; Tibetan momos; Vietnamese banh mi; endless varieties of wraps; and, extending the ever more popular hand foods just a bit, Korean chicken wings. We live in the age of variety—though many of these choices are already branding, franchising, and aiming to be as universally available as the golden arches. At which point, will they become the new version of nachos or General Tso's chicken—a supposedly ethnic tradition invented here?

> Side Dish <

Vegetarian and Vegan

Vegetarianism is a familiar and common practice in some parts of the world, such as South Asia, where a variety of religious beliefs rule out killing and eating animals. In the United States, advocates began writing about and arguing for the practice in the mid-nineteenth century, but it was often seen as an odd or fringe belief. In the 1960s and 1970s vegetarianism found new support among young people, who opened restaurants such as Moosewood near Cornell University in Ithaca, New York (*Moosewood Cookbook* is one of the ten bestselling cookbooks ever), Greens in San Francisco, and Spring Street Natural in New York City. In the twenty-first century vegetarianism has found new and widespread popularity. Some object on ethical or moral grounds to killing animals at all or to raising animals for slaughter under brutal conditions, as the industrial system of meat production requires. There are people who think eating a vegetarian diet is healthier for your body, and those concerned about climate change who point to the environmental cost of, for example, cutting down forests to create cattle pastures. Seeing increased interest in meatless meals, companies small and large have developed meat-like substitutes that are now available in every supermarket and are featured on a wide variety of restaurant menus. With so many choices, vegetarianism has gone from being seen as a sign of oddness or eccentricity to being a normal and expected choice.

Veganism is a more recent movement that rejects eating or using any animal products on the grounds that animals should not be exploited by humans. The term was invented in 1944. Unlike vegetarians, vegans reject eating eggs, dairy products, and honey.

"Milk" without Cows—Old and New

Digestion and health, religious practices, and, more recently, ethical and environmental concerns have all led people to seek alternatives to cow's milk. Until the process of "pasteurizing" (named after the French scientist Louis Pasteur, who invented a way to sterilize milk with heat) was created in the 1860s, fresh milk was often filled with harmful bacteria. The safest ways to eat it were in the forms of cheese, butter, or yogurt—all created through processes that would kill off the bacteria. Even so, while infants can drink cow's milk, more than 60 percent of the world's adults have difficulty digesting it.

It is possible to use a great variety of plants to make something that resembles milk but does not upset people's stomachs: most grains (including rice and oats), legumes (soy, peas, peanuts), nuts (several of the well-known varieties such as almonds or walnuts), and seeds (chia, sesame, flax). The many choices of "milk" in the dairy case have their own long—and short—histories.

At one time observant Catholics were not allowed to eat either meat or milk during a variety of special moments throughout the calendar that add up to about one hundred days. In medieval Europe almond milk was a common, although expensive, substitute, especially in cooking. It has a pleasant flavor, is thinner than cow's milk, and was often sweetened. Almonds only grew well in the Mediterranean parts of Europe and were in great demand, particularly during Lent, the forty days before Easter. Muslims also living near the Mediterranean have used almond milk at least since the 1200s.

Coconut milk is made by grating and pressing the white "meat" of coconuts and is different from the "water" naturally produced within the coconut. Because it is created by people, cooks can adjust how thick and creamy the "milk" is to suit the individual dish they are preparing. Beginning in Southeast Asia and then brought to the Pacific Islands and on to the Americas, coconut milk is a familiar ingredient in many world cuisines. Oat milk, by contrast, is a very recent addition to the dairy case. It was invented in 1994 by two Swedish brothers who recognized that most people worldwide have difficulty digesting cow's milk. Milk has gone from being a shared drink of common experience to being the start of an ever-growing set of choices and alternatives.

HOW THIS BOOK CAME ABOUT

I first learned of Paul's food-and-history research when Marina Budhos and I were writing *Sugar Changed the World*. In his book *Out of the East*, Paul explained that sugar was considered a spice or medicine in medieval Europe and that spices were never used to disguise the taste of meat that had gone bad (a common food-history myth). Spices were costly; a noble who could afford them could far more easily send out a huntsman to bring back fresh meat whenever necessary. Paul responded graciously to some questions, and then I enjoyed reading two later books of his: *American Cuisine* and *Ten Restaurants That Changed America*. I approached him about working on a book together and was thrilled that he liked the idea.

As we discussed the concept of a book that would get at American history through key meals and moments, we were drawn to the idea of including the voices and perspectives of people with direct knowledge of some of the food cultures we intended to explore. We worked with a team of consultants—Tatum Willis and David Zheng from Yale, Amanda Palacios from New Mexico State University, and Dr. Frederick Douglass Opie of Babson College. Each contributed to and helped to guide our research in the area of his or her own particular knowledge. The dual tracks of learning through research (books, articles, scholarly studies) and shared personal experience was rich and rewarding. Our book is far better because of the insights and stories our contributors shared with us. We see this book as an invitation to readers to explore the vast cornucopia of food and history for all peoples. Begin your own quest! As you will see, there are so many surprises awaiting you.

Here's one personal story of my own: exchanging emails with Tatum, I learned about the importance of huckleberries in salmon feasts. That struck an odd chord. While I was growing up in Manhattan, every so often my parents would take me for a special treat to Steinberg's on Broadway, between 81st and 82nd Street. Steinberg's was a Jewish dairy restaurant. Observant Jews do not mix milk with meat, so some restaurants specialize in meat (no butter, no milk) and others in dairy (no meat). We were not religious, but the kreplach (dumplings, often filled with a slightly sweet cheese) and blintzes there were delicious. I distinctly recalled that you could order a red, white, and blue combination plate (cheese, cherry, and blueberry blintzes), but I would ask if I could have huckleberry. Could that be true? Why would a fruit associated with the Mountain West appear on the menu of a dairy restaurant on Manhattan's Upper West Side?

Paul was first drawn to writing about contemporary food

when he saw an exhibit of a collection of historical menus gathered at the New York Public Library. Searching that collection (now available online), I did indeed find one from Steinberg's, and listed under "Specials" were FRESH HUCKLEBERRY BLINTZES. I may never know how huckleberries reached that kitchen or whether the restaurant was just using a fun term for a tasty, available filling (huckleberry pie is also on the menu), secure in the knowledge that no huckleberry expert would ever arrive to dispute their language. But there it was—Tatum's recollection of a Cayuse salmon feast in the Pacific Northwest linked to my childhood special meal on the other side of the continent. Food tells so many stories that can connect us.

CITATIONS

This book was written in a series of stages. Marc and Paul wrote an early draft, then sent it to the four contributors along with specific questions. Tatum, Amanda, and David then added their insights, either in writing or in extended interviews. Tatum also provided reference books. Dr. Opie sent many links and connections to primary sources to enhance "his" chapters. Marc and Paul incorporated this new material and followed up on leads the contributors provided. They then sent back a revised draft for comments. This process was repeated after the in-house editor sent her notes and questions. In this last round Dr. Opie offered both reference leads and editorial suggestions. We wanted to capture that rich exchange and collaborative work process for readers. The notes listed here record the ebb and flow of personal and reference resources. Then, page by page, we listed the source for specific quotations and concepts.

Introduction

p. ix: "apple pie": Rossi Anastopoulo, "Why American Pie Isn't So American After All," FOOD52, October 8, 2021, food52.com/blog/24688-apple-pie-origin-story.

p. ix: For a detailed description of what is known about the three days of Thanksgiving feasting in Plymouth Colony in 1621, see James Deetz and Patricia Scott Deetz, *The Times of Their Lives; Life, Love, and Death in Plymouth Colony* (New York: W. H. Freeman, 2000), 6–9.

p. ix: "eel": Nicole L. Elmer, "Eel. It's What's for (Thanksgiving) Dinner," The University of Texas at Austin Biodiversity Center, November 15, 2021, biodiversity.utexas.edu/news/entry/eel-for-thanksgiving.

For a more humorous but still informative animation about eel and Thanksgiving, see Drew Christie, "A Thanksgiving Eel," *New York Times*, November 18, 2021, nytimes.com/video/opinion/100000001905852/a-thanksgiving-eel.html.

Chapter 1

pp. 3–4: We have long known that people had arrived in the Americas by at least thirteen thousand years ago because we have found a distinctive kind of carved-stone spear point in many parts of North America that can be dated to that period—which was also when the ice sheets were melting enough to allow people to cross into and through the continent. But in the past thirty years or so we have found evidence—of many types—that people arrived here earlier, even though ice did seem to block entry. Strangely, some of the oldest sites are far south, in Chile, for example, meaning that people would have had to come a long way over time to get there. This suggests that people first arrived by water, hugging the coastline and traveling south on the edge of the Pacific. Most recently DNA studies and careful analysis of Native languages suggest that there were several groups who migrated to the Americas perhaps as early as twenty-five thousand years ago—some survived, some intermarried with later groups, some left only faint traces. As far as we know now, there were a variety of "First Americans"—we are beginning to learn about waves of different peoples coming from Asia through Siberia, perhaps mixing there or on the way, and then arriving here: pulses of movement, settlement, and mixture. Some scholars, though, question and dispute all of these early dates. This is a very exciting arena of historical investigation with, right now, more questions than answers.

Dr. Jennifer Raff weighs the genetic and physical evidence for the peopling of the Americas and concludes that the early dates and coastal routes are likely in her book *Origin: A Genetic History of the Americas* (New York: Twelve, 2022), 267–276.

Marc is a fan of archaeologica.org, which posts articles on archaeological discoveries as they become available, as often as several times a week. These "hot-off-the-presses" pieces are what one set of experts asserts or a journalist summarizes, and then may be challenged or debated by others. Here are a few posts about the peopling of the Americas that give a sense of the current state of knowledge and the nature of the debates:

Clovis points and dating: Charles C. Mann, "The Clovis Point and the Discovery of America's First Culture," *Smithsonian Magazine*, November 2013, smithsonianmag.com/history/the-clovis-point-and-the-discovery-of-americas-first-culture-3825828/.

Possible East Asian origins of some First Americans: Cell Press, "DNA from Ancient Population in Southern China Suggests Native Americans' East Asian Roots," *ScienceDaily*, July 14, 2022, sciencedaily.com/releases/2022/07/220714145052.htm.

Claim of genetic history of First Americans: Jennifer
Raff, "A Genetic Chronicle of the First Peoples in the
Americas," *SAPIENS*, February 8, 2022, sapiens.org/
archaeology/ancient-dna-native-americans/.

First migration: Louise Franco, "Ancient Humans Might
Have Settled in South America over 18,000 Years
Ago After Discovery of Chromosomes," *Nature World
News*, August 18, 2022, natureworldnews.com/
articles/52610/20220818/ancient-humans-settled
-south-america-over-18-000-years-ago.htm.

Possible evidence of humans in the Americas over thirty
thousand years ago: University of Texas at Austin,
"New Mexico Mammoths Among Best Evidence for
Early Humans in North America," Phys.org, August 1,
2022, phys.org/news/2022-08-mexico-mammoths
-evidence-early-humans.html.

Study that challenges these early dates: University of
Wyoming, "Study Challenges Theories of Earlier Human
Arrival in Americas," Phys.org, April 20, 2022, phys.org/
news/2022-04-theories-earlier-human-americas.html.

p. 4: Marc interviewed Tatum on June 17, 2022, and she then led us to
other valuable resources that contributed to this chapter; a second
interview took place on September 9, 2022. Books Tatum shared
with us are noted with a (TW) below.

pp. 4–12: Introduction to the CTUIR, including history, culture, and
food in their own words:

"A Brief History of CTUIR," Confederated Tribes of the
Umatilla Indian Reservation, ctuir.org/about/brief
-history-of-ctuir/.

"First Foods & Life Cycles," Confederated Tribes of the
Umatilla Indian Reservation, ctuir.org/about/first
-foods/.

pp. 4–12 A PowerPoint on the Cayuse with Native singing, historical photos, and maps: "Liksiyu: The Cayuse People—Confederated Tribes of the Umatilla Indian Reservation," Jaguar Bird, posted November 4, 2020, YouTube video, youtube.com/watch?v=JPHg2SDCBMw.

pp. 4–12: Museum on the reservation that is owned and run by members of the CTUIR with a video on Lewis and Clark from a Native point of view: Bobbie Conner and Bill Lang, "Video Presentation: Foreigners in Native Homelands: Lewis and Clark and the Pioneers," Tamástslikt Cultural Institute, tamastslikt.org/video-presentation-foreigners-in-native-homelands-lewis-and-clark-and-the-pioneers/.

pp. 4–12: For the long history of Native peoples in this area, see Katrine Barber, *Death of Celilo Falls* (Seattle: University of Washington Press, 2005), 20. (TW)

p. 5: For the quoted text about Wishpoosh, see Laura Gibbs, "Origin of the Tribes: Chinook," Mythology and Folklore UN-Textbook, mythfolklore.blogspot.com/2014/06/pacific-nw-origin-of-tribes.html. Tatum pointed out that Coyote stories such as this one are only told in the fall, which would be the proper time to recount it, but she shared the story, which of course appears in a book that may be read at any time, as it perfectly illustrates the connection between each Native group and its particular area of land. There is an extensive, rich, and thoughtful discussion of the question of sharing with outsiders in *They Are Not Forgotten* (cited below). The authors acknowledge that some respected elders "oppose the writing, recording, and documenting of the Sahaptin, Cayuse, Nez Perce languages, as well as teaching of them in classrooms." Some feel that "place name are family-based intellectual property that should only be passed to their own descendants." The creators of the book rather feel that what they have recorded and shared affirms that "Indian people occupied the land and that they used and enjoyed it—indeed, they possessed and owned it." It is in that same spirit that we included a small part of the Wishpoosh story. See p. xiii for this important discussion.

Eugene S. Hunn, et al., *Cáw Pawá Láakni/They Are Not Forgotten: Sahaptian Place Names Atlas of the Cayuse, Umatilla, and Walla Walla* (Pendleton, Oregon: Tamástslikt Cultural Institute, 2015), Ictixec quotation, 29; Jim Yoke recollection, xv; Morning Owl quotation, 7–8. (TW)

p. 6: Celilo as center of trade: Barber, *Death of Celilo Falls*, 22.

pp. 6–11: Video and text on Celilo Village: Iona Frank, "Scenic Outlook of the Columbia River and Celilo Village," PocketSights, pocketsights.com/tours/place/Scenic-outlook-of-the-Columbia -River-and-Celilo-Villlage-63251:7037.

p. 6: For Beavert, see Virginia R. Beavert, *The Gift of Knowledge/ Ttnúwit Átawish Nch'inch'imamí: Reflections on Sahaptin Ways* (Seattle: University of Washington Press, 2017). (TW) The author was the recipient of the Washington Governor's Heritage Award and the coauthor of a dictionary of the Yakama language.

pp. 6–7, 10–11: The story of the damming of the falls is fully explored in Barber, *Death of Celilo Falls*; for the longer history of dam projects on the Columbia, see 30–34.

pp. 7–8: The Tommy Thompson account we used as a source came to us this way: Tatum encouraged us to contact the Columbia Gorge Discovery Center and Museum, which led Marc to interview Susan Buce (June 21, 2022), who manages their collection of artifacts. Susan in turn told Marc about Martha Ferguson McKeown, *Come to Our Salmon Feast* (Portland, Oregon: Binfords & Mort, 1959), a children's book that was helpful in crafting this chapter. The author also appears in the film listed below of the last feast before the dam, where she is identified as the only non-Native person who has been "adopted" into the Wy-am, one of the groups holding the ceremony. (For more on the Wy-am and the dam, see Nicole

Greenfield, "The Celilo Wy'am Are Still Here," Natural Resources Defense Council, Inc., March 10, 2021, nrdc.org/stories/celilo -wyam-are-still-here.)

pp. 7–8: For images of the falls, see Wasco County Historical Museum, *Celilo Falls: Remembering Thunder; Photos From the Collection of Wilma Roberts* (The Dalles, Oregon: Wasco County Historical Museum Press, 1997).

pp. 7–8: Film of the last First Salmon Feast before the construction of the Celilo Falls dam: Gathering the Stories, "Last Salmon Feast at Celilo. Oregon Historical Society film, 1957," Facebook, February 6, 2016, facebook.com/gatheringthestories/videos/last-salmon -feast-at-celilo-oregon-historical-society-film-1957/ 1111061052238874/.

pp. 7–8: Historical photos of the Celilo First Salmon Feast: Thomas Robinson, "Gallery: Feast of the First Salmon," Confluence, June 27, 2019, confluenceproject.org/library-post/gallery-feast-of-the -first-salmon/.

pp. 7–8: Barber, *Death of Celilo Falls*, 22–24 on the history and importance of the First Salmon ceremony at Celilo.

pp. 8–9: Marc's interview with Janice Jones was conducted on September 9, 2022.

p. 9: For Meriwether Lewis on camas resembling "lakes," see Susan Kephart, "Camas," the Oregon Encyclopedia, oregonencyclopedia .org/articles/camas/.

pp. 9–10: Tatum's interviews with Judith Moses and Kanim Moses were included in a text she sent to Marc on June 23, 2021.

For debates over the dam, Native testimony, and payments to Native groups, see Barber, *Death of Celilo Falls*, 64–95 and 155–82.

p. 11: For E. Thomas Morning Owl's quotation on Native people strengthening themselves and also *The Ghosts of Celilo*, see Bob Hicks, "Actor and composer Thomas Morning Owl from 'The

Ghosts of Celilo,'" *The Oregonian*, March 4, 2011, oregonlive.com/performance/2011/03/actor_and_composer_thomas_morn.html.

p. 11: For the Biden administration and the possibility of breaching four dams, see Mark Walker and Chris Cameron, "Plaintiffs in Long Fight Over Endangered Salmon Hope a Resolution Is Near," *New York Times*, August 15, 2022, nytimes.com/2022/08/15/us/politics/salmon-dams-washington.html.

pp. 11–12: The Kanim Moses quotation is from the interview with Tatum cited on p. 137.

Chapter 2

pp. 15-24: The historical background for this chapter can be found in Alvin M. Josephy, Jr., ed., *America in 1492: The World of the Indian Peoples Before the Arrival of Columbus* (New York: Alfred A. Knopf, 1992), especially "Chapter 4: Taking Care of the Earth and Sky" by Peter Iverson, which discusses the Southwest; "Chapter 5: Farmers of the Woodlands" by Peter Nabokov with Dean Snow, which discusses Cahokia; "Chapter 6: Men of Maize" by Miguel León-Portilla, about Mesoamerican corn culture; and "Chapter 12: American Frontiers" by Francis Jennings, which describes the corn cultures of the Southwest and the interactions of Mesoamerican peoples with Natives from other regions.

pp. 15-16: Charles C. Mann, *1491: New Revelations of the Americas Before Columbus* (New York: Alfred A. Knopf, 2005), especially "Chapter 6: Cotton (or Anchovies) and Maize (Tales of Two Civilizations, Part I)," which gives various then-current views on how corn was created.

This article gives the more recent understanding of how corn was developed that we use in the text: "Ancient DNA Continues to Rewrite Corn's 9,000-Year Society-Shaping History," Smithsonian Institute, December 14, 2020, si.edu/newsdesk/releases/ancient-dna-continues-rewrite-corns-9000-year-society-shaping-history.

p. 17: On varieties of corn: Maricel E. Presilla, *Gran Cocina Latina: The Food of Latin America* (New York: W. W. Norton & Company, 2012), the section on corn, 233–57; quotation, 234.

p. 17: For the importance of blue corn to Native peoples in the Southwest, see Janice Goodwin and Judy Hall, "Healthy Traditions, Recipes of Our Ancestors" (Grand Forks, North Dakota: National Center for Native American Aging), 12, nrcnaa.org/pdf/cookbook.pdf.

pp. 17–18: For some newer views on Cahokia, including questions on why it was abandoned:

Glenn Hodges, "Why Was the Ancient City of Cahokia Abandoned? New Clues Rule Out One Theory," *National Geographic*, April 12, 2021, nationalgeographic.com/environment/ article/why-was-ancient-city-of-cahokia-abandoned-new-clues -rule-out-one-theory.

Markus Milligan, "New Insights into Monks Mound at Cahokia," *Heritage Daily*, July 21, 2022, heritagedaily.com/2022/07/new -insights-into-monks-mound-at-cahokia/144180.

pp. 18-20: For information on the Pueblo and especially the Three Sisters and agriculture, this PowerPoint from the Albuquerque Museum is clear and useful: cabq.gov/artsculture/albuquerque -museum/casa-san-ysidro/documents/museum-lesson-pueblo -agriculture.pdf.

p. 19: For the Acoma massacre in 1599, see Wisconsin Historical Society, "Trial of the Indians of Acoma, 1598," American Journeys, americanjourneys.org/aj-104/summary/.

pp. 18-20: For teachers or librarians who would like to develop lessons around a Pueblo-based understanding of Native encounters with the Spanish, this can be a very useful tool: Christine P. Sims, "First Encounters with Spanish Explorers: A Pueblo Experience," Indian Pueblo Cultural Center, indianpueblo .org/wp-content/uploads/SIMS_First_Encounters_with_ Spanish_Explorers_LP2.pdf.

pp. 19–20: For the background to and the story of the 1680 revolt, see "The Pueblo Revolt of 1680," New Mexico Nomad, newmexiconomad.com/the-pueblo-revolt-of-1680/.

pp. 19–20: For the first-person account of Po'Pay's vision and promises used in our text, see James E. Seelye, Jr. and Steven A. Littleton, eds., "'As They Had Been in Ancient Times': Pedro Naranjo Relates the Pueblo Revolt, 1680," in *Voices of the American Indian Experience, Volume 1: Creation–1877* (Santa Barbara, California: ABC-CLIO, LLC, 2013), 74.

pp. 20–22: Amanda's initial description of her family and food came on February 27, 2021; she approved the current version on August 12, 2022.

Amanda's description of the flavor and texture of dried corn: Amanda Palacios to Marc Aronson, April 24, 2023.

pp. 21–22: For the story of Dr. Fabian Garcia and the Hatch chile, see Maricel E. Presilla, *Peppers of the Americas: The Remarkable Capsicums That Forever Changed Flavor* (Berkeley, California: Ten Speed Press, 2017), 159–63. Includes several pages of photos of chiles.

Also useful: Dave Dewitt, "New Mexico Chile History," Hatch Chile Store, hatch-green-chile.com/pages/new-mexico-chile-history.

pp. 23–24: For how nachos were invented, see Pati Jinich, "The Original Nachos Were Crunchy, Cheesy and Truly Mexican," *New York Times*, October 29, 2020, nytimes.com/2020/10/29/dining/nachos-recipes.html.

pp. 23–24: For the story of nachos and *Monday Night Football*, see Ted Berg, "How Howard Cosell Helped Bring Nachos to the World," *USA Today*, November 13, 2013, ftw.usatoday.com/2013/11/how-howard-cosell-helped-bring-nachos-to-the-world.

Chapter 3

pp. 29–36: For historical background on food, the dinner, and New Orleans:

Elizabeth M. Williams, *New Orleans: A Food Biography* (Lanham, Maryland: Rowman & Littlefield, 2013).

Charles-César Robin, *Voyages to Louisiana 1803–1805*, trans. Stuart Omer Landry, Jr. (New Orleans: Pelican Publishing Company, 1966).

Pierre Clément de Laussat, *Memoirs of My Life to My Son During the Years 1803 and After, Which I Spent in the Public Service in Louisiana as Commissioner of the French Government for the Retrocession to France of That Colony, and Its Transfer to the United States*, trans. Agnes-Josephine Pastwa (Baton Rouge: Louisiana State University Press, 1978).

For African American foodways, history, and culture, we relied on three main texts as well as suggestions from Dr. Opie:

Frederick Douglass Opie, *Hog and Hominy: Soul Food from Africa to America* (New York: Columbia University Press, 2008).

Jessica B. Harris, *High on the Hog: A Culinary Journey from Africa to America* (New York: Bloomsbury, 2011). There is also a Netflix television series based on the book and starring Dr. Harris.

Adrian Miller, *Soul Food: The Surprising Story of an American Cuisine, One Plate at a Time* (Chapel Hill: University of North Carolina Press, 2013).

p. 29–30: For "balbancha," see Shane Lief and John McCusker, "Chapter Two: Balbancha," in *Jockomo: The Native Roots of Mardi Gras Indians* (Jackson, Mississippi: University Press of Mississippi, 2019); and Daniel Usner, "Balbancha: How American Indians Kept New Orleans in their Homeland," NOETC Inc, posted September 27, 2018, YouTube video, youtube.com/watch?v=iirzpm5EJzI.

An argument to change the name of the city back to the Native version: Paul Schmelzer, "Bulbancha Forever: From NOLA to

Minneapolis, a Movement to Revitalize Indigenous Names Grows," The Ostracon, January 4, 2021, theostracon.net/bulbancha -indigenous-naming-jeffery-darensbourg/.

pp. 30–31: For France giving Louisiana to Spain as a result of the Seven Years' War, see Fred Anderson, *Crucible of War: The Seven Years' War and the Fate of Empire in British North America, 1754–1766* (New York: Alfred A. Knopf, 2000), 505.

pp. 30–31: For the idea of the Franco-Spanish republic, see W. J. Eccles, *France in America* (New York: Harper & Row, 1972), 230.

pp. 31–32: For the Michaux story, see Stephen E. Ambrose, *Undaunted Courage: Meriwether Lewis, Thomas Jefferson, and the Opening of the American West* (New York: Simon & Schuster, 1996), 70–71.

p. 32: For background on Haiti's fight for independence, see Marc Aronson and Marina Budhos, *Sugar Changed the World: A Story of Magic, Spice, Slavery, Freedom, and Science* (New York: Clarion Books, 2010), 87–90.

pp. 32–33: On the role of Haitian independence in the Louisiana Purchase, see Marshall Smelser, *The Democratic Republic: 1801–1815* (New York: Harper & Row, 1968), 89–93.

p. 32: For "'wall of brass,'" see "Treaty of San Ildefonso," The Napoleon Series, napoleon-series.org/research/government/ diplomatic/c_ildefonso.html.

p. 32: For Thomas Paine's suggestion of sending free African Americans to Louisiana, see James V. Lynch, "The Limits of Revolutionary Radicalism: Tom Paine and Slavery," *The Pennsylvania Magazine of History and Biography* 123, no. 3 (1999): 177–99.

pp. 33–35: On gumbo: Stanley Dry, "A Short History of Gumbo," Southern Foodways Alliance, southernfoodways.org/interview/ a-short-history-of-gumbo/.

pp. 33–34: On African gumbos: Opie, *Hog and Hominy*, 11.

p. 34: On okra and the origin of its name: Harris, *High on the Hog*, 17; on gumbo: Harris, *High on the Hog*, 105-6.

p. 34: Opie, Harris, and Miller all stress how African American cooks, whether under enslavement in big plantation kitchens or on small farms, preparing foods for white or Black people, as well as during segregation and after, both called on, shared, or recalled African techniques and traditions and made creative use of whatever they had available to them. Dr. Opie returned to this theme in his notes on the manuscript sent on August 20, 2022.

Chapter 4

pp. 37, 39-46: Very little African history is taught in our schools. Instead we offer folktales, stories of enslavement, and then the heroism of Nelson Mandela. That gives a picture of Africa as "primitive" or "traditional," "enslaved and colonized," and freed through one sterling individual. In reality, over thousands of years peoples throughout Africa developed complex societies with their own pageants of history and enjoyed centuries of rich contact with Asia, with Europe, and, after 1492, with the Americas. For example, the Bantu migration, a world historical event that transformed much of Africa, is never mentioned in standard K-12 curricula. (See Mark Cartwright, "Bantu Migration," World History Encyclopedia, April 11, 2019, worldhistory.org/Bantu_Migration/.) A first step in correcting the absence of African history is to look at food.

All three of our key experts stress that Africans arrived in the Americas with knowledge of some Americans foods and spices and their own creative adaptations of them. They specifically reject the idea that Africans were disoriented or overwhelmed by the foods and ingredients they encountered.

On the African background of African American cooking (and the insight that Africans were already using American products before arriving here): Opie, *Hog and Hominy*, 1-15.

On the African background of African American cooking: Harris, *High on the Hog*, 5-20.

On African cooking being African American before 1619: Miller, *Soul Food*, 13.

Dr. Opie sent his initial notes for this chapter on July 3, 2021; his comments on the revised text arrived August 20, 2022. Dr. Opie gave us links to useful primary sources that are cited by our page numbers below; his suggestions are identified by (FDO).

p. 39: Fishing in Africa: Opie, *Hog and Hominy*, 51.

p. 39: For information on Africans in the Southwest, see Carroll L. Riley, "Blacks in the Early Southwest," *Ethnohistory* 19, no. 3 (1972): 247-60.

For DNA study on American cattle: Floriday Museum of Natural History, "Ancient DNA Reveals African Roots of American Cattle," Florida Musem of Natural History, August 10, 2023, https://scitechdaily.com/ancient-dna-reveals-african-roots-of -american-cattle/.

For African cattle ranchers: Dr. Russell Moul, "America's First Cowboys Were Likely Enslaved Peoples, New Analysis Reveals," IFL Science, September 29, 2023, www.iflscience.com/americas -first-cowboys-were-likely-enslaved-peoples-new-analysis -reveals-70922.

pp. 39-41: On fish and fish fry: Miller, *Soul Food*, 70-90.

p. 39: For the Mendes quotation, see Helen Mendes, *The African Heritage Cookbook* (New York: Macmillan, 1971), 79. (FDO)

p. 40: For the McHatton-Ripley quotation, see Eliza McHatton-Ripley, *From Flag to Flag: A Woman's Adventures and Experiences in the South During the War, in Mexico, and in Cuba* (New York: D. Appleton and Company, 1889), 138. (FDO)

p. 40: For Elizabeth Henry, see Federal Writers' Project: 1936– 1940, "American Life Histories," Louisiana folder, 1024, Robert McKinney interview with Elizabeth Henry [African

American born 1873], "Queen of Fish Fries," January 11, 1939.
(FDO)

pp. 40–41: For Zora Neale Hurston, see Marjorie Kinnan Rawlings, *Cross Creek Cookery* (New York: Charles Scribner's Sons, 1942). (FDO)

p. 41: For the large 1937 fish fry, see Mary A. Poole, "Alabama Deep Sea Fishing Rodeo," November 5, 1937, p. 1, Box A 13, file Alabama Cities & Towns, Mobile Cuisine, Work Progress Administration (State Records), the Manuscript Division of the U. S. Library of Congress Archives, Washington, D. C. (FDO)

p. 41: On Africans, African Americans, and hot sauce, see Miller, *Soul Food*, 208–21; for "glass of Maunsell White," see Miller, *Soul Food*, 217.

p. 41: On Lilly Harris Dean: Amelia Nierenberg, "Overlooked No More: Lillian Harris Dean, Culinary Entrepreneur Known as 'Pig Foot Mary,'" *New York Times*, November 27, 2019, nytimes .com/2019/11/27/obituaries/lillian-harris-dean-overlooked.html.

p. 42: For a history of macaroni and cheese as an African American dish, see Miller, *Soul Food*, 129–45.

p. 42: For Langston Hughes, see Opie, *Hog and Hominy*, 90.

p. 43: For Dew Drop Inn menu, see Opie, *Hog and Hominy*, 106.

p. 43: For Baraka, see Opie, *Hog and Hominy*, 133.

p. 43: For Grosvenor, see Opie, *Hog and Hominy*, 134.

p. 44: For Ali, Jackson, and Brown chain restaurants, see Opie, *Hog and Hominy*, 136.

p. 44: For health concerns on deep-fat frying, see Miller, *Soul Food*, 85.

p. 44: For the Jeffries quotation, see Opie, *Hog and Hominy*, 136.

pp. 45–46: For the myth of the origin of the name "hush puppy," see Miller, *Soul Food*, 198.

Chapter 5

pp. 47, 49–53: Basic sources for this chapter are:
James McWilliams, *A Revolution in Eating: How the Quest*

for Food Shaped America (New York: Columbia University Press, 2005).

Keith Stavely and Kathleen Fitzgerald, *America's Founding Food: The Story of New England Cooking* (Chapel Hill: University of North Carolina Press, 2004).

Chapter 6

pp. 60–63: Dr. Opie sent a collection of clippings from African American newspapers related to soda fountains and to segregation that are indicated below with (FDO) to us on July 3, 2021.

pp. 55–57: On the history of carbonation: "The History of Sparkling Water," Borg & Overström, August 26, 2022, borgandoverstrom .com/en/blog/the-history-of-sparkling-water/.

p. 57: On A. T. Stewart and the department store: Marc Aronson, *Four Streets and a Square: A History of Manhattan and the New York Idea* (Somerville, Massachusetts: Candlewick Press, 2021), 104–7.

pp. 57–58: Wikipedia has a useful history of the pharmacy in the United States, wikipedia.org/wiki/History_of_pharmacy_in_the_ United_States. As ever, this is a good starting place, but it is worth following their notes to see the sources used.

pp. 58–60: General histories of soda fountains:

Jan Whitaker, "Lunching at the Drug Store," Restauranting through history, September 20, 2020, restaurantingthroughhistory.com/tag/soda-fountains/.

Mary Bellis, "The History of the Soda Fountain," ThoughtCo, September 21, 2019, thoughtco.com/history-of-the-soda -fountain-1992432.

p. 59: For Sir John's description, see Fred Ferreti's "A Remembrance of Soda Fountains Past," *New York Times*, April 27, 1983. https://timesmachine.nytimes.com/timesmachine/1983/04/27/ 125496.html?pageNumber=55.

p. 59: On Coca-Cola and cocaine: NIDA Blog Team, "Did Coca-Cola

Ever Contain Cocaine?," Just Think Twice, justthinktwice.gov/
article/did-coca-cola-ever-contain-cocaine.

pp. 59–60: On the early name and formula for 7UP: Meredith Cooper,
"The Untold Truth of 7UP," Mashed, January 24, 2023,
mashed.com/206921/the-untold-truth-of-7up/.

pp. 60–63: For soda fountains, segregation, and civil rights, see:
Greg Bond, "Drugstores and the Color Line: Remembering
Pharmacies as Sites of the Civil Rights Movement," History News
Network, February 10, 2021, historynewsnetwork.org/article/179149.

Ameer Hasan Loggins, "The Little Known History of Black
Women Using Soda Fountains as Contested Spaces," African
American Intellectual History Society, May 8, 2017, aaihs.org/the
-little-known-history-of-black-women-using-soda-fountains-as
-contested-spaces/.

pp. 60–61: Thomforde's is a fascinating case that deserves more
research. It is mentioned as a kind of "home" in Harlem—for
example, in a December 4, 1948, article by Hazel Sharper
in the *New York Age* (an African American newspaper), and
Malcolm X's pleasure at dining there was recalled by a Harlem
activist who worked at Thomforde's (see "Thomforde's 'The
Best Ice Cream' Shop Harlem, NY 1903–1983," *Harlem World*,
harlemworldmagazine.com/thomfordes-best-ice-cream-shop
-harlem-ny-1903-1983/). Several sources mention that when
Harlem exploded and white-owned businesses on 125th Street, the
center of Harlem, were targets of criticism and rage, Thomforde's
was left alone. But it was white owned, segregated for its first
twenty years, and closed in the eighties when employees joined a
union and went on strike, given their terribly low wages. Dr. Opie
suggests caution in accepting word of how well liked it was, which
again suggests that further research is needed on why some did
so appreciate it and the conflict between its role in Harlem and
its treatment of African American workers. Our thanks to Auburn

Nelson, reference librarian at the Schomburg Center for Research in Black Culture, for finding several pieces in the *Amsterdam News*, the leading Harlem newspaper, that related to Thomforde's.

On Thomforde's segregated history: Les Matthews, "Workers Strike Thomforde's," *New York Amsterdam News*, August 8, 1981, proquest.com/hnpnewamsterdamnews/docview/226520287/CEA4B9B63D694D92PQ/17?accountid=35635.

On Thomforde's closing: "Board to Hear Charges on Schools, Thomforde," *New York Amsterdam News*, December 26, 1981, proquest.com/hnpnewamsterdamnews/docview/226432440/CEA4B9B63D694D92PQ/22?accountid=35635.

On opposition by restaurant to unionization: "Little State Agency Packs a Big Wallop," *New York Amsterdam News*, November 14, 1981, proquest.com/hnpnewamsterdamnews/docview/226402724/CEA4B9B63D694D92PQ/21?accountid=35635.

On low salaries before the strike: "The Tattler," *New York Amsterdam News*, September 12, 1981, proquest.com/hnpnewamsterdamnews/docview/226476377/CEA4B9B63D694D92PQ/19?accountid=35635; and "Meeting on Thomforde's," *New York Amsterdam News*, August 22, 1981, proquest.com/hnpnewamsterdamnews/docview/226479665/CEA4B9B63D694D92PQ/18?accountid=35635.

On how Thomforde's was protected during riots: "A ray of hope seen in Thomforde's strike," *New York Amsterdam News*, November 7, 1981, proquest.com/hnpnewamsterdamnews/docview/226453050/CEA4B9B63D694D92PQ/20?accountid=35635.

p. 61: For Sidney Barthwell, see "Sidney Barthwell Sr. '29: A Legend of Black Pharmacy Entrepreneurship," Wayne State University, February 1, 2022, cphs.wayne.edu/news/sidney-barthwell-sr-29-a-legend-of-black-pharmacy-entrepreneurship-44244.

p. 61: For Robert Shauter, see "Shauter Drug Co.," Case Western Reserve University, case.edu/ech/articles/s/shauter-drug-co.

p. 61: For Lionel Hampton, see "Lionel Hampton Back at Paradise," *Michigan Chronicle*, May 8, 1943, 18. (FDO)

pp. 61–62: For gobbles at a soda fountain, see Helen Johnson, "Girl Who Cheats Herself on Food Must Pay Penalty," *Atlanta Daily World*, February 22, 1940. (FDO)

p. 62: For white druggists, see "Won't Sell Sodas," *Afro-American*, July 16, 1920. (FDO)

p. 62: For Pauli Murray and the Howard protests, see Patricia Bell-Scott, *The Firebrand and the First Lady: Portrait of a Friendship: Pauli Murray, Eleanor Roosevelt, and the Struggle for Social Justice* (New York: Alfred A. Knopf, 2016), 113–17.

pp. 62–63: For Dockum and the successful protests led by teenagers, see:

"Dockum Drug Store Sit-In," Kansas Historical Society, June 2011, kshs.org/kansapedia/dockum-drug-store-sit-in/17048.

Steve Hill, "Sixty Years Ago, Teenagers in Wichita Started a Movement," *Humanities* 39, no. 4 (2018), neh.gov/article/sixty -years-ago-teenagers-wichita-started-movement.

p. 63: For the Katz's protest, see Noah Lawrence, "Since it is my right, I would like to have it: Edna Griffin and the Katz Drug Store Desegregation Movement," *The Annals of Iowa* 67, no. 4 (2008), iowaculture.gov/history/education/educator-resources/primary -source-sets/iowa-leader-civil-rights-and-equality/it-my.

Chapter 7

pp. 67–72: Basic background for this chapter:

Cindy R. Lobel, *Urban Appetites: Food and Culture in Nineteenth-Century New York* (Chicago: University of Chicago Press, 2014).

Richard Pillsbury, *From Boarding House to Bistro: The*

American Restaurant Then and Now (Boston: Unwin
Hyman, 1990).

pp. 67–68: The role of Russo-German wheat farmers in America
and the connection between American wheat being shipped to
the world and cheap steerage tickets being available for European
immigrants coming to America is explored in Scott Reynolds
Nelson, *Oceans of Grain: How American Wheat Remade the
World* (New York: Basic Books, 2022).

pp. 67–68: Basic information on German immigration, with images:
"The Germans in America," European Reading Room, April 23,
2014, loc.gov/rr/european/imde/germchro.

p. 68: Thomas Nast and Santa Claus: Lorraine Boissoneault, "A Civil
War Cartoonist Created the Modern Image of Santa Claus as
Union Propaganda," *Smithsonian Magazine*, December 19, 2018,
smithsonianmag.com/history/civil-war-cartoonist-created
-modern-image-santa-claus-union-propaganda-180971074/.

pp. 69–70: World War I and name changes of German foods: Jeff
Morgan, "When Sauerkraut Became 'Liberty Cabbage,'" *Medium*,
February 19, 2018, medium.com/iowa-history/when-sauerkraut
-became-liberty-cabbage-bb84f4369d52.

p. 72: On "'delicore'" and the new uses of Jewish delis: Maggie
Hennessy, "The Old-School Deli Is the Newest Hot Girl Hangout,"
Bon Appétit, September 22, 2022, bonappetit.com/story/
katz-new-york-delis-fashion-delicore.

Chapter 8

p. 73: The Oliver Wendell Holmes quotation used in the chapter title
can be found in *The Rumford Kitchen Leaflets*, which are digitized
and available here: curiosity.lib.harvard.edu/women
-working-1800-1930/catalog/45-990064284800203941.

pp. 73, 75–83: This chapter draws on research Paul did for Paul
Freedman, *American Cuisine: And How it Got This Way* (New

York: Liveright Publishing Corporation, 2019), including especially "Chapter 5: Why Americans Welcomed Industrial Food"; and for Paul Freedman, *Ten Restaurants That Changed America* (New York: Liveright Publishing Corporation, 2016).

p. 75: For foods that first appeared at the 1893 fair, see:

> Melanie Linn Gutowski, "8 Quintessential American Products That Debuted at the 1893 Chicago World's Fair," Ancestry, September 4, 2014, blogs.ancestry.com/cm/8-quintessential-american-products-that-debuted-at-the-1893-chicago-worlds-fair/.

> Ellen Shubart, "5 Fun Facts about the World's Columbian Exposition of 1893," Chicago Architecture Center, architecture.org/news/historic-chicago/5-fun-facts-about-the-worlds-columbian-exposition-of-1893/.

> Katherine Nagasawa, "From Vienna Beef to PBR: Five Food and Drink Legacies of the 1893 World's Fair," NPR, May 22, 2019, npr.org/local/309/2019/05/22/725421470/from-vienna-beef-to-p-b-r-five-food-and-drink-legacies-of-the-1893-world-s-fair.

p. 75: For Nancy Green, see Katherine Nagasawa, "The Fight to Commemorate Nancy Green, the Woman Who Played the Original 'Aunt Jemima,'" NPR, June 19, 2020, npr.org/local/309/2020/06/19/880918717/the-fight-to-commemorate-nancy-green-the-woman-who-played-the-original-aunt-jemima.

pp. 75–76: For the Rumford Kitchen, see Freedman, *American Cuisine*, 184.

pp. 76–77: The racialized aspects of scientific nutrition and the specifics of the focus on beef can be found in Rachel Laudan, *Cuisine and Empire: Cooking in World History* (Berkeley: University of California Press, 2013).

p. 76: For *Mrs. Beeton's*, see Laudan, *Cuisine and Empire*, 255.

pp. 76–77: "'Those races'": Laudan, *Cuisine and Empire*, 256.

p. 77: "emperor of Japan": Laudan, *Cuisine and Empire*, 256.

p. 77: Chinese exclusion and rice eating: Laudan, *Cuisine and Empire*, 257.

pp. 77–78: For scientific nutrition, see PFAC 179–87.

p. 79: "'still eating spaghetti'": Freedman, *American Cuisine*, 178.

p. 79: "'I'd rather eat'": Freedman, *American Cuisine*, 181.

pp. 79–80: Anyone who wants to explore further on food, race, nutrition—could you eat your way to improvement, or did your race define how you would eat?—should see Nicholas J. P. Williams, "Becoming What You Eat: The New England Kitchen and the Body as a Site of Social Reform, " *The Journal of the Gilded Age and Progressive Era* 18, no. 4 (2019): 441–60.

p. 80: "'chief minister'": Laudan, *Cuisine and Empire*, 253.

p. 80: For "'the application of the principles of chemistry'" and to learn more about the Rumford Kitchen, see "The Rumford Kitchen," Rumford, August 1999, rumford.com/RumfordKitchen.html.

p. 80: "'Fletcherizing'": Freedman, *American Cuisine*, 181.

p. 81: "'Wonder Bread'": Freedman, *American Cuisine*, 174.

Chapter 9

This chapter draws on research Paul did for *Ten Restaurants That Changed America*, especially "Chapter 5: Mamma Leone's: Italian Entertainment," 171–208.

pp. 85–86: For Bertolotti's (with a photo), see Rick Beard and Leslie Cohen Berlowitz, eds., *Greenwich Village: Culture and Counterculture* (New Brunswick, New Jersey: Rutgers University Press, 1993), 265.

pp. 86, 89: To estimate the cost of meals in modern dollars, we used: Ian Webster, "$0.15 in 1905 is worth $5.13 today," CPI Inflation Calculator, in2013dollars.com/us/inflation/1905?amount=0.15.

"The Relative Worth of," Measuring Worth,
measuringworth.com/dollarvaluetoday/
?amount=50&from=1906#.

p. 86: For John Reed, his poem, heterodoxy, and the Village
Bohemians, see Aronson, *Four Streets and a Square*, 210–21.

p. 88: "Gonfarone's": Freedman, *Ten Restaurants*, 185.

p. 90: "'Mother, for you'": Freedman, *Ten Restaurants*, 190.

p. 91: For pizza in Pompeii: Elizabeth Polovedo, "A Proto-Pizza
Emerges from a Fresco on a Pompeii Wall," *New York Times*, June
27, 2023 (updated June 29, 2023).

Chapter 10

pp. 97–103: This chapter draws on research Paul did for *Ten
Restaurants That Changed America*, especially "Chapter 4:
Howard Johnson's: As American as Fried Clams," 129–70.

p. 98: "'serve the finest'": Freedman, *Ten Restaurants*, 130; "'when
you sit'": Freedman, *Ten Restaurants*, 175.

pp. 101–102: For food trucks, see:

Eleonor Segura, "A Brief History of the Good Humor
Ice Cream Truck," *MotorTrend*, March 19, 2021,
motortrend.com/vehicle-genres/good-humor-ice
-cream-truck-history/.

"Our History," Good Humor, goodhumor.com/us/en/our
-history.html.

"History of Food Trucks and How They've Shaped
America," Prestige Food Trucks, March 23, 2020,
prestigefoodtrucks.com/2020/03/history-of-food
-trucks-and-how-theyve-shaped-america/.

Chapter 11

pp. 105–115: David sent his initial notes and comments on July 8,
2021, and expanded his thoughts on October 6, 2022.

This chapter draws on research Paul did for *Ten Restaurants That Changed America*, especially "Chapter 6, The Mandarin: 'The Best Chinese Food East of the Pacific,'" 209–50. The statistic on the number of Chinese restaurants appears in Freedman, *Ten Restaurants*, 209, and Freedman, *American Cuisine*, 265–69.

p. 111: Michelle Zauner, *Crying in H Mart: A Memoir* (New York: Alfred A. Knopf, 2021. Reprinted 2023), 8.

Chapter 12

p. 120: For information on hunger, see "Hunger in America Statistics," *The Barbecue Lab*, March 2023, thebarbecuelab.com/hunger-in -america/.

pp. 124–125: For milk without cows, see:

Cory Stieg, "How Oatly Went from a Decades-Old Obscure Brand to a $10 Billion IPO," CNBC, May 20, 2021, cnbc. com/2021/05/20/oatly-ipo-how-the-swedish-oat-milk-became -popular-in-us.html.

Benjamin Kemper, "Nut Milks Are Milk, Says Almost Every Culture Across the Globe," *Smithsonian Magazine*, August 15, 2018, smithsonianmag.com/history/nut-milks-are-milk-says -almost-every-culture-across-globe-180970008.

For a breakdown of plant milks, see "Which Plant Milk Is Best for You," *Consumer Reports*, September 2022, 11.

AUTHORS AND CONTRIBUTORS

Marc Aronson has been an editor, author, and publisher of books for younger readers for more than thirty years. As an editor he created the first international and multicultural YA imprint, EDGE, and as an author he was the first winner of the Robert F. Sibert Award for nonfiction for *Sir Walter Ralegh and the Quest for El Dorado*. *Sugar Changed the World: A Story of Magic, Spice, Slavery, Freedom, and Science*, which he wrote with his wife, Marina Budhos, was his first venture into the fascinating crossing point of food and history. He has a PhD in American history from NYU and is an associate professor of professional practice at Rutgers University, where he trains future youth librarians.

Paul Freedman is the Chester D. Tripp professor of history at Yale University, where he specializes in medieval social history. He is the author of *American Cuisine: And How It Got This Way*, *Ten Restaurants That Changed America*, and *Out of the East*: *Spices and the Medieval Imagination*, and he is the editor of *Food: The History of Taste*, which was honored with an award from the International Association of Culinary Professionals.

Frederick Douglass Opie is a professor of history and foodways at Babson College, where he teaches courses such as African History and Foodways, African American History and Foodways, and Food and Civil Rights. He is the author of *Hog and Hominy: Soul Food from Africa to America*. He also hosts a food history blog: fredopie.com/food.

Amanda Palacios is from El Paso, Texas. She completed a bachelor of arts at the University of Texas in Middle Eastern languages and cultures with a minor in anthropology, and a master's at New Mexico State University in anthropology with a minor in food studies and a graduate certificate in public health. She plans to do work and research on addressing health issues and food access in the border region.

Tatum Willis is an enrolled member of the Confederated Tribes of the Umatilla Indian Reservation (CTUIR) and also descends from the Yakama, Nez Perce, and Oglala Lakota peoples. A graduate of Yale University, she is currently a managing director of Cayuse Mission Solutions, part of the Cayuse family of companies.

David Zheng is an artist and filmmaker. After growing up in China, he immigrated to South Carolina and later attended Yale University. His passion for cooking got him started in food history, and he is especially interested in the history of Chinese cuisine.

INDEX